Basics of Assessment

A Primer for Early Childhood Educators

Oralie McAfee, Deborah J. Leong, and Elena Bodrova
Research Fellows, National Institute for Early Education Research

National Association for the Education of Young Children
Washington, DC

NAEYC wishes to thank the authors, who donated many, many hours to this project.

Cover and inside illustrations by David Clark
Photographs and figures provided by the authors, unless credited otherwise

National Association for the Education of Young Children
1509 16th Street, NW
Washington, DC 20036-1426
202-232-8777 or 800-424-2460
www.naeyc.org

Through its publications program the National Association for the Education of Young Children (NAEYC) provides a forum for discussion of major issues and ideas in the early childhood field, with the hope of provoking thought and promoting professional growth. The views expressed or implied are not necessarily those of the Association.

Carol Copple, publications director. Bry Pollack, senior editor.
Malini Dominey, production and design. Natalie Cavanagh, editorial associate.

Library of Congress Control Number: 2004107686
ISBN: 1-928896-18-9
NAEYC Item #257

About the Authors

Oralie McAfee, professor emerita of early childhood education at Metropolitan State College of Denver, is author of numerous publications related to working with young children and their families, and has done research on assessment practices and needs in Head Start and in selected state-funded prekindergarten programs.

Deborah J. Leong is a professor of psychology at Metropolitan State College of Denver and a research fellow at the National Institute for Early Education Research (NIEER) where she is working on a computerized pre-K state standards database and a database of preschool assessment instruments with Elena Bodrova. She has written on assessment, play, early literacy, and the development of self-regulation in young children.

Elena Bodrova is a senior researcher at Mid-continent Research for Education and Learning (McREL) in Aurora, Colorado, and a research fellow at NIEER. Previously, she had been visiting professor of educational psychology at Metropolitan State College of Denver, senior researcher at the Russian Center for Educational Innovations and the Russian Institute for Preschool Education, and adjunct professor of educational psychology at Moscow Teacher Training College. She writes extensively on early literacy, play, and assessment.

The authors have collaborated on a number of other projects together, including McAfee and Leong on *Assessing and Guiding Young Children's Development and Learning,* 3d ed. (Allyn & Bacon, 2002), and Leong and Bodrova on both *Tools of the Mind: The Vygotskian Approach to Early Childhood Education* (Merrill/Prentice Hall, 1996) and four educational videos (Davidson Films).

Contents

List of Boxes

Acknowledgments

We wish to acknowledge the support of the National Institute for Early Education Research (NIEER)*, Rutgers University, and particularly Steve Barnett, in the development of this booklet.

Thanks to Amy Enninga, Nicole Babb, Judy Edwards, and the Jefferson County (Colorado) Head Start.

Thanks to Linda Espinosa, University of Missouri; John Kendall, Mid-continent Research for Education and Learning (McREL); and Heather Holmes-Lonergan, Metropolitan State College of Denver.

We appreciate the help and encouragement of Carol Copple, Bry Pollack, and NAEYC in preparation and publication.

We especially appreciate the many children, colleagues, and families with whom we have worked and who helped us develop our understanding of child assessment and its uses in improving the education of young children.

---

* The National Institute for Early Education Research (NIEER), an organization established by Pew Charitable Trusts and other funders, is part of a broader pre-K initiative designed, funded, and managed by the Trusts to improve the quality of early childhood education. Led by Susan Urahn, the Trusts' early education initiative demonstrates the Trusts' commitment to the young children of this country. NIEER conducts and commissions research, analyzes the policy implications, and communicates the knowledge base needed to ensure that educational opportunities made available for 3- and 4-year-old children are of high quality. NIEER's goal is to help influence those decisions by providing objective, unbiased, research-based information to state and federal policymakers, journalists, researchers, educators, and others making decisions about early childhood programs. NIEER resources can be accessed at www.nieer.org.

About This Booklet

As an early childhood educator, you probably have your own ways of appraising children's development and learning that seem to work—things you have done in the past, things you are doing now. But in today's environment—where *assessment* is a term much bandied about and where questions, claims, and concerns arise from families, supervisors, and policymakers—you may be looking for help to make sense of what you hear and are expected to do. Specifically, you want to confidently

• assess children in sensible, meaningful ways,

• describe to families the kinds of assessment you are using and why, and share with them the resulting information and insights about their child, and

• use information from assessment to benefit children's learning and development.

Purpose and audience

This booklet will help whether you are new to assessment's terms and approaches or want a quick refresher to reinforce your understanding and commitment.

The intended audience is teachers working with 3- to 8-year-olds, with an emphasis on prekindergarten and kindergarten. Many of the basic principles apply to assessing younger children, too. But we leave discussion of infant and toddler assessment to others with expertise in that area, some of whom are listed in the FOR MORE INFORMATION section.

Basics of Assessment won't tell you everything you need to know about this subject. Instead, we describe the basic concepts and vocabulary of child- and classroom-oriented assessment in today's achievement-focused environment. We leave out many details and how-tos of assessment, such as learning to observe, setting up and organizing a classroom to support assessment, and

---

The Responsibility to Assess

From the joint position statement of NAEYC and the National Association of Early Childhood Specialists in State Departments of Education:

Policymakers, the early childhood profession, and other stakeholders in young children's lives have a shared responsibility to . . . make ethical, appropriate, valid, and reliable assessment a central part of all early childhood programs. To assess young children's strengths, progress, and needs, use assessment methods that are developmentally appropriate, culturally and linguistically responsive, tied to children's daily activities, supported by professional development, inclusive of families, and connected to specific, beneficial purposes: (1) making sound decisions about teaching and learning, (2) identifying significant concerns that may require focused intervention for individual children, and (3) helping programs improve their educational and developmental interventions. (NAEYC & NAECS/SDE 2003, 1)

---

developing a portfolio system. For these and other assessment specifics, see any of the excellent guides listed in FOR MORE INFORMATION.

In this booklet we focus primarily on the assessment of children in typical classroom settings for the purpose of supporting their development and learning. We hope to convey the many positive things that can happen during, and as a result of, sound, sensitive, systematic assessment of children's development and learning. Not the least of these can be teachers who feel more efficient and effective working with young children.

Even though "we cannot 'know' a child in any final sense" (Almy 1959, 217), we can know children well enough to support their learning, know them well enough to convey to others their strengths and needs, and know a group well enough to create a good place for each child to grow and learn.

Reader-friendly features

Webster's defines *primer* as "a small introductory book on a subject," and *Basics of Assessment* is exactly that. It's certainly small, only 8½ inches square and barely a hundred pages long. Like any good primer, it uses what we hope is clear and nontechnical language to explain assessment's purposes, processes, and tools. It also includes the following:

On-the-spot definitions. Occasionally a shaded box pops up adjacent to a term highlighted in the text, where a passage uses an assessment term we think you may be unfamiliar with. Some of these highlighted terms are explained and discussed in later chapters; all reappear in the GLOSSARY, sometimes with more extended definitions.

Boxes. The boxed sidebars take a closer look at topics related to or mentioned in the main text. But you don't have to stop and read them to understand that text. If you do skip over them, though, be sure to return later, as they contain significant assessment information on their own. Use the LIST OF BOXES to find them.

Lots of examples. Throughout we offer concrete examples in several forms. Classroom vignettes and samples of children's actual work help translate abstract concepts and approaches into experiences you can identify with from your own classroom. Excerpts from standards documents, assessment guides, and assessment forms acquaint you with the tools of assessment. (The forms reproduced as figures are offered not as models or ideals but as samples of typical materials. Their inclusion does not imply endorsement of any particular curriculum or assessment approach.)

Glossary. Lately it seems that the terms used to label and describe what we do when we assess have sprouted like dandelions in the spring. And like dandelions, just as you think you have grasped one and made it yours, another shows up. This in mind, we include a GLOSSARY, which covers all the terms defined in those shaded boxes plus many more that a classroom teacher is likely to encounter.

Resources. Finally, we recognize that comprehensive discussion of subjects such as observation, portfolios, and planning is beyond the scope of this booklet. The annotated FOR MORE INFORMATION section points you to publications and Web sites where more assessment information is available.

Getting Acquainted with Assessment

A Definition

Assessment is the basic process of finding out what the children in our classroom, individually and as a group, know and can do in relation to their optimum development and to the goals of the program. With that knowledge of those children, we can plan appropriate curriculum and effective instructional strategies to help them develop and learn, monitoring their progress along the way.

In the current climate you are likely to hear the term *assessment* used for almost any type of appraisal of young children for a range of purposes. Many people use the term loosely, as a broad label for any and all of the varied ways we might determine "where a child is" in development and learning—maybe a vocabulary test, a brief observation, a fine motor skills checklist, a diagnostic reading test, or a height and weight measurement.

But assessment as described in this booklet has a more specific meaning: *Assessment is the process of gathering information about children from several forms of* **evidence**, *then organizing and interpreting that information.*

As this basic definition makes clear, sound child assessment is not based on a single measure.

> **evidence**—An outward sign or indication. In child assessment, this would be an indication of a child's development or learning.

standardized test—A test specially constructed according to a set of testing standards (see AERA/APA/NCME 1999). It requires a trained examiner to administer and interpret its scores.

The use of **standardized tests** in the early childhood classroom is controversial. Standardized test results should never be the sole form of evidence we look at. Too many factors make it difficult to use standardized tests with young children successfully (more on this in a later section). In some situations a standardized test can contribute useful information, but one or even several such tests alone would not constitute adequate assessment of young children.

Fortunately, everyday classroom experiences present many opportunities for children to demonstrate their development and learning. For example, we can appraise a child's oral language development by listening to her converse with other children in a variety of work and play situations, talking with her informally, checking on her contributions to group discussions, evaluating her ability to follow oral directions, seeing whether other adults can understand her, and asking her to point to or name pictures on a worksheet. Again, any one of these individual assessments would not provide enough evidence on its own.

Meaningful child assessment always involves our looking at information from multiple sources gathered over time before drawing conclusions about a young child's development and learning.

Deciding *why* we are assessing is the critical first step in the assessment process (see the section THE PROCESS OF ASSESSMENT). A look at all the important objectives we can meet with assessment highlights why it is so fundamental to good teaching (see WHY WE ASSESS YOUNG CHILDREN). But any assessment, however well-intentioned, serves children only when it is soundly constructed and sensitively administered (see SOUND ASSESSMENT IS . . .).

The push for systematic assessment and the focus on achievement are great these days. But child assessment is not something new and wholly different for early childhood educators. We have always observed children, talked with them about what they were doing, noted interesting and unique things they did and said, recorded their accomplishments in development and learning, and shared information with families.

The Process of Assessment

Think of the process of assessment as a cycle of interrelated, basic decisions. The cycle begins with how we answer the first, critical question:

- What is our purpose for assessment?

For that purpose, then,

- What area or areas of children's development and learning should we assess?
- When is the appropriate time to assess?
- How can we gather information about what children know and can do?
- What does the information we gather mean?
- What use do we make of the information?

This cycle gives us a systematic way of thinking about assessment, of making adjustments as we go in light of our results. It is a way of understanding where and how assessment fits into a good program for helping young children develop and learn.

Why We Assess Young Children

Asked why they do assessment, many early childhood educators might answer, "Because it's expected and required." That is often true, but there are four even more important reasons why we might assess young children.

To monitor children's development and learning

We assess to find out "where children are" in any particular aspect of their growth, development, and learning—individually or as a group, at that moment and over time. For example,

> Where do this child's skills at letter recognition stand in relation to the goals of our program?

> How are these children doing compared with what we know about typical physical development for 7- and 8-year-olds?

> Some of the children started the year having trouble sharing; how have they been doing lately?

These snapshots of growth and learning over time help us identify and anticipate children's strengths and needs. We cannot effectively plan and tailor a program to build on those strengths and meet those needs without this vital information.

To guide our planning and decision making

We use the information we gather about these specific children in this specific classroom to guide our planning and decision making—that is, what books to read; what activities, experiences, and materials to provide; what instructional strategies to use. For example,

> If we find that some of the children have difficulty recalling and talking about the main events in a story they have just heard, we plan learning activities to help them.

> If we find that Amy cannot play and work with others without constant conflict, we figure out things to do to help her learn to get along.

> If the children have large motor skills beyond what we expect for their age but are way behind in the fine motor control necessary for school tasks, we devise interesting ways to help them develop eye-hand coordination and control of finger, hand, and arm muscles.

To identify children who might benefit from special services

The early childhood years are often the occasion for hearing, vision, and immunization checks as well as for identification of possible speech and language impairment, emotional disturbance, physical disabilities, developmental disabilities, and other conditions that call for special services. Initial identification of a possible problem might come from the teacher, from an alert parent, or through **screening.** If a potential problem is detected, the next step is a referral for an in-depth appraisal by a specialist or team of specialists who determine whether special services are needed, and if so, develop a plan to assist the child. For example,

> Buddy was not talking at all in the classroom, so his teacher referred him to a specialist for an in-depth evaluation.

> Ling's vision screening prompted the school nurse to suggest to her parents that Ling be checked by an eye doctor.

screening—A brief, relatively inexpensive, standardized procedure designed to quickly appraise a large number of children to find out which ones should be referred for further assessment.

To report to and communicate with others

Some assessment information is collected to be shared among specialists, educators, and researchers. As classroom teachers, we must be familiar with assessment concepts and practices in order to understand what specialists and researchers are saying and to make useful the important evidence about children we have accumulated day after day.

Some assessment information is to be shared with families and community members. We must be able to explain assessment concepts and results to them in everyday language. All early childhood educators need to know and be able to explain why assessing young children's development and learning is far more than just giving a test.

Assessment information is also used for **program evaluation** and for **accountability** (e.g., to determine whether the program meets state or federal mandates regarding student achievement). Classroom teachers might help to collect information for those purposes, especially when evidence from classroom-based assessments such as those described in this booklet is required. Sometimes the assessment is done by outside evaluators or specialists.

Sound Assessment Is . . .

A sound and appropriate assessment process has several essential features. Among the most important are that its assessments are reliable and valid, free of bias, and suited to children's developmental characteristics.

Sound assessment is reliable and valid

An assessment is *reliable* when it measures accurately and consistently. The procedure would yield similar results if repeated or if done by different people. Assessment results may be unreliable if the child being assessed found the questions or tasks vague or confusing or if the child was distracted, uncomfortable, or ill, or was just guessing at an answer.

An assessment is *valid* when it measures what we want to measure and not something else. When assessment is valid, the results agree with other information gathered in other ways about the same behavior. Because it is impossible to capture the whole of what a child knows or can do, assessment can only sample that whole. To be valid, assessment of a child's knowledge or skills must include enough samples to accurately represent that larger whole. Assessment of something simple, such as a child's skill at cutting with scissors, requires us to collect only one or a few pieces of evidence to be valid. We need

more evidence for a valid assessment of anything more complex, such as a child's cognitive development.

Publishers of standardized tests—e.g., California Achievement Test, DIAL-3 (Development Indicators for the Assessment of Learning, 3d ed.), and Early Screening Inventory—provide reliability and validity statistics on their tests in ways specified by measurement specialists (see AERA/APA/NCME 1999). Teachers and administrators can determine whether such a test has been judged reliable and valid by reading published test reviews, which function as a kind of "consumer report" for testing. (See FOR MORE INFORMATION for several sources of reviews.)

The child assessment that we do every day in our classrooms is not required to meet such rigorous standards. But teachers must take responsibility for knowing how to evaluate the reliability and validity of assessments, as well as how to increase their reliability and validity as needed (e.g., by collecting more evidence, using a different method, using uniform methods).

Sound assessment is free of bias

Sound assessment gives each child, regardless of that child's experience, status, or background, as good a chance as any other child to show what he or she knows and can do. Assessment that does not do that contains **bias** or is said to be "biased."

Standardized tests are often criticized for being biased against one group or another, but classroom assessments that teachers create and do can also be biased. No teacher intends to bias an assessment, but it is likely to happen unless we guard against it. For example,

> We may draw faulty conclusions from observing children's participation in a given activity because we give boys (or girls) more opportunity to participate.

> We may assume knowledge of urban (or rural) life that children do not have; then we ask questions related to a passage about a taxicab (or tractor), putting the children who lack experience with that thing at a clear disadvantage.

bias—Any characteristic of an assessment that unfairly discriminates against a child or a group of children on the basis of factors such as gender, urban or rural residence, socioeconomic status, family structure, ethnic origin, culture, and language.

We may be unable to look beyond our own attitudes to see a child as he or she really is; we decide that Ernesto is "pushy" because he insists on being in the front at storytime, and our bias against pushy children keeps us from noticing that Ernesto is nearsighted.

Bias on the basis of language and cultural differences or disability is a significant enough problem that teachers and programs may be required by policy or law to address it. Bias is especially important to consider when using a standardized test, because teachers may not be allowed to reword or even repeat its questions.

Language and cultural differences

Many children come to classrooms from homes where language, culture, and valued knowledge differ from those of the school and those of their teacher. We must give special thought to assessing these children due to the likelihood of underestimating what they know and can do.

The results of our assessment of such children may not be accurate for a wide variety of reasons. Most obvious, of course, is that the assessment is in English when the child is not fluent in that language. Even when we assess in the child's preferred language, problems can still arise. A Spanish version of a standardized test, for example, may not use the dialect of Spanish the child is familiar with. Or children may know the name of an object in English, but because the test is given in their home language they may assume they are to answer in that language. Or children may use all their knowledge of sounds, regardless of language, as one child did:

> Luis was shown pictures of objects and asked to say the beginning letter sound of the name of the object, in this case a bed. He replied "k." Fortunately the teacher spoke Spanish, and realized that Luis was thinking of *cama,* the Spanish word for bed.

Children's prior cultural knowledge and experience may be quite different from what we expect. Children may have had limited opportunity to learn about things we assume "everyone" knows—football, television programs, holidays, advertisements, celebrities. Or they may have their own set of culturally important experiences. For example,

A child in a Chicago classroom who is asked "Which is an activity we do in the winter?" might pick a picture showing a family at the beach because winter is when her family goes home to Mexico.

It is in such instances that a teacher's being able to ask for an explanation—"Tell me more" or "Explain that"—can lead to better assessment. Often problems occur when we try to interpret, rather than investigate, the lack of an answer or an incorrect answer. For example,

When Sylvia is unsure about an answer she says, "I don't know," stares blankly at the teacher, or looks away. If her teacher knew that such guessing is discouraged as a form of communication in Sylvia's family, she would interpret Sylvia's behavior differently.

These issues arise with children at all ages. But they are especially serious with young children, who tend to be less familiar than are older children with the culture and language of school.

Be Sensitive to the Impact of Language and Cultural Differences

Seek help and information from someone who knows the language and customs of the families you are working with.

Use multiple assessment measures, checking one against the other. Set up assessment situations so children can demonstrate their capabilities in a supportive context and in a wide variety of ways.

Rephrase directions, requests, and questions so children can understand.

Ask for explanations that might give you a clue to the child's thinking.

Assume some gap, if cultural and language differences are great, between what the child knows and can do and what he or she can demonstrate in the classroom.

Distinguish deficits or disabilities from these language, cultural, ethnic, and social differences.

Focus on whether the child applies the concept correctly, no matter what language the child uses.

Special needs

In assessing children whose individual differences require them to have special help, most teachers have the assistance of a specialist or team from their district or the community. Assessing children with disabilities may require you to make accommodations or modifications to the specific assessments you use or to your overall assessment process.

Accommodations are changes in assessment materials, procedures, or settings to eliminate barriers related to a child's disability that keep children from demonstrating what they know and can do. For example, a child with an emotional or learning disability might be given extra time, the assessment might be done in two parts, or the child might go into a separate room where there are no distractions. A child who is deaf might get an interpreter. A child with poor vision might get large-print books.

Modifications are changes in assessment materials or procedures that may alter what the assessment measures or the comparability of its results. For example, in assessing reading comprehension, a passage might be read *to* a child, rather than read *by* the child as the assessment was designed.

There are no clear or definite answers to the question of how to fairly assess what children with special needs know and can do. The concern is greatest when the assessment information is going to be used beyond the classroom or school—e.g., for accountability to the state (Olson 2004).

Be Aware of Assessment-Related Law

Certain laws and regulations guide assessment of children with disabilities in schools that accept federal money. These laws are designed primarily to protect the rights of children and their families; periodically updated, the laws provide good guidance for assessment of all children.

The guidance we outline in this booklet (e.g., using multiple measures, involving families, ongoing performance assessment) supports the recommended approaches to assessment.

For a thoughtful and complete explanation of these laws, see the Council for Exceptional Children's (1999) publication *IDEA 1997: Let's Make It Work*.

Sound assessment is developmentally appropriate

We cannot get trustworthy information about young children unless we take into account what they are like. Understanding the value of assessing young children is fairly straightforward. But doing it well is difficult, given the challenges that are typical for this age group.

Uneven development

Young children develop and learn in spurts, plateaus, and even what seem to be steps backward before going forward again. What a child could not do two weeks ago she may have mastered today and not display tomorrow. Some children develop in leaps and bounds; others take tiny but steady steps.

An individual child's development may be uneven, with his social, physical, language, and intellectual development seemingly on different time lines.

Young children may show their emerging development in different ways. Some may demonstrate learning in what they say or write; others may express learning more fully in their drawings, constructions, or movement.

Limited language skills

Young children vary in their ability to understand and express ideas. For example, they may be unable to follow directions because they don't understand the words, because they remember only the last few words, or because they are simply overwhelmed by too many words. And they may be unable to respond because their vocabulary is limited or because they have trouble forming intelligible sounds.

Sensitivity to context

Young children are highly sensitive to the context of assessment—the *physical setting* where the assessment occurs (classroom, playground, lunch-room; available equipment and materials), the *people involved* (familiar teacher, parent, stranger; small group, large group, one-on-one), and the *activity* (listening to a story, group discussion, making a graph).

Every teacher is familiar with a child who volunteers nothing in the classroom but never stops talking with friends on the playground. This is context at work—for that child, the classroom context discourages talking; the playground context encourages it.

Children are most likely to perform to the best of their ability in a familiar setting, with known and trusted adults, in an activity they find interesting. But even in a familiar situation with a familiar adult, direct questioning may cause some young children to become uneasy and unresponsive. If children are from a culture where that type of adult-child interaction is not typical, they are even less likely to show their true capabilities.

Limited interest in being assessed

Encouraging children to do their best often motivates older children. But it likely will be lost on younger ones, as the idea of "doing their best" may have no meaning for them.

> [Young children] have limited interest in being assessed—an adult's agenda—especially when the assessment procedures interfere with their normal range of movement, talk, and expression of feelings. (Hills 1992, 46)

Assessment is more likely to be trustworthy and to produce meaningful results when it meshes with children's own interests and desires.

Inability to meet the demands of certain types of tasks

Group-administered, paper-and-pencil, multiple-choice tasks are a particularly poor fit with young children. Children are easily distracted and they may have trouble marking responses, proceed at a pace different from the teacher's, lose their place, misunderstand directions, or choose a response that makes sense to them but is not the desired answer. For example,

A kindergartner is to circle the picture of the correct response on a worksheet, following directions read by the teacher. She takes too long on the first line and is still working on her decision when the teacher moves on. Engrossed in the task, she pays no attention to the directions for the second line and tries to apply directions for the third line to the second line. By now she is hopelessly lost but still trying. She applies snatches of the directions. She hears something about green, and circles a green garbage can. . . . You get the idea.

Because the task was inappropriate, it revealed nothing about her knowledge.

Handle Assessment Information with Care

When we assess we often collect and record sensitive information about children and families. In sharing this information with other people, we should be ethical and professional.

Discuss results only with those who have a right and need to know, that is, with the child's parents or guardians, school or center administrators, and other teachers and specialists who work with the child. Don't share the information with your friends and family or as casual conversation anywhere.

Don't describe children using labels. Concentrate on describing what children know and can do and on devising ways to help them improve. Rapidly growing and developing young

children are ill-served by being labeled by their teachers—as "ADHD" (attention deficit hyperactivity disorder), "hyper," "shy and withdrawn," "over-achiever," "Asperger's." Children with disabilities are usually better served by keeping focused on what they *can* do instead of on their disability.

Keep confidential any files containing sensitive information about family background or children's problems, and discuss that information only on a professional basis. Never make potentially damaging remarks either orally or in writing.

Model and teach ethical behavior related to confidentiality to classroom assistants and volunteers. Be consistent in your own practice.

Doing Assessment

Assessment in the Classroom

By now you may have a general understanding of what the term *assessment* means, why young children might be assessed, and what sound assessment is and is not.

Now let's turn to the actual "doing" of *child assessment*—but not just any child assessment. The remainder of this booklet focuses on assessment used by teachers in classrooms on a day-to-day basis—*classroom assessment* (sometimes termed *classroom-embedded assessment*)—mainly for the purposes of supporting children's development and learning and guiding our planning and decision making.

The kind of classroom assessment most suitable for teachers of young children is called *performance assessment*, which means that we appraise children's development and learning as it is demonstrated in the course of tasks the children "perform" in everyday classroom life, or as close to everyday as possible.

Specifically, performance assessment refers to the *type of response* by the child. To check on motor coordination, for example, we see whether a child moves in a coordinated fashion. To assess social interaction, we observe children playing, working, and talking together. To assess reading, a child reads; writing, a child writes.

For example, you have made a performance assessment when:

> You note that a child devises a workable solution to dividing a limited number of manipulatives between himself and his buddies.

> You make and use a chart on which you record how a group or an individual child spends the classroom day.

> You give a child a direction involving two steps, being careful to give no visual clues, and then make a record of your directions and what the child did.

In performance assessment we might pose questions or tasks designed explicitly as appraisals of what children know or can do (*structured performances*). For example, we might ask children to run an obstacle course—something they wouldn't naturally do in the course of everyday life.

But as much as possible, we should try to make our performance assessment *authentic.* The authenticity of an assessment refers to the *situation or context* in which the child performs the task as well as what the child is asked to do. In **authentic assessment,** the children apply their knowledge and skills in a situation or to a task that is meaningful to them and is within the range of typical classroom activity. Sometimes such occasions arise spontaneously, and we take advantage of them as fruitful opportunities to see what children know and can do. Sometimes we arrange for occasions to occur, for example, by asking the child who is today's snack helper to "put *one* napkin at each place" as an assessment of her understanding of one-to-one correspondence. When performance assessment is authentic, it is not set apart from learning.

Now let's turn to what and why we might assess; how to gather and make sense of evidence of children's learning and development; and then what to do with what we have learned.

authentic assessment— A type of assessment that uses tasks as close as possible to real-life practical and intellectual challenges in a real-life context.

Basics of Assessment

What Can (and Should) Be Assessed

Young children are fascinating and complex beings, offering us no end of interesting things to study. For classroom purposes it is essential that we assess two aspects of children's development and learning:

• the major child growth and development domains

• the expected outcomes for children as a result of the program—that is, of our curriculum and teaching

Although the two are interrelated, we discuss growth and development domains and expected outcomes separately to make sure they are both assessed.

Assessing major growth and development domains

Any and all domains of children's learning and development can be assessed. How individual elements of those domains are grouped into categories and the labels those categories are given can vary from program to program. Here is one typical grouping:

Cognitive or **intellectual domain**—Children's ability to talk about, think about, and describe the world around them. Ability to solve problems, see relationships, classify, describe likenesses and differences. Complexity of their constructions, dramatic play, and the like. This cognitive domain also includes young children's acquisition of skills and understandings in content areas such as mathematics, science, social studies, reading, and writing. Children's language development and use might be assessed as part of the cognitive domain or as a separate area.

Affective or **social-emotional domain**—Children's ability to relate to other children and adults, to take the perspective of another, to resolve conflicts, to cooperate. Attitudes toward school and learning, interests. Ability to regulate their own behavior, pay attention when that is needed, focus on an activity long enough to complete it. Self-confidence, willingness to try new things. Moral development.

Physical or **psychomotor domain**—Children's physical being, such as health, eye-hand coordination and fine muscle development. Gross and fine motor control of the body. Strength and stamina to walk, run, climb, play.

Other groupings are possible. A program might devise other or additional categories to emphasize what it views as important; for example, children's creative expression, habits of mind, or approaches to learning.

Looking at the whole child

We can use categories, such as those above, to talk about how children develop and learn; they help us focus on particular areas. But developmentally appropriate programs for young children look at the *whole child* and work to promote development in all the domains. So it follows that assessment in developmentally appropriate programs should gather information on a broad range of what children know and can do.

Children's functioning in any one domain is important in its own right and is important to development and functioning in other domains. If we assess in only one or two areas, we lack useful information to support children's development in other areas. For example,

> A child who is unable to work and play cooperatively with other children (affective domain) is likely to have a tough time learning science in a group project (cognitive domain).

A child who cannot control his body (physical domain), and so frequently bumps into other children, may have difficulty being accepted socially (affective domain).

Assessment across the domains also is important to ensure that we do not miss any significant gaps in children's progress. Unless we assess broadly, children may be making strides in one or two domains but failing to progress in other areas without our recognizing it. For example, we need to find out whether some of the children in a group (perhaps even the group as a whole) are acquiring social skills but not getting the phonemic awareness skills they need to become competent readers, or vice versa.

Assessing expected outcomes for children

Expectations for what children should know and be able to do as an outcome of a program are typically captured in written form (e.g., in a document or guide), and these outcome statements are called a variety of different names. Very often they are called **standards.** (But they might instead be called "learning expectations," "criteria," "desired results," "goals and objectives," "early learning standards.")

standards—A statement that specifies what children should know and be able to do.

States may develop outcome statements for their early childhood education programs, as may local education and community agencies. The federal government and foundations may develop outcome statements for programs receiving funding. Specific programs such as Head Start have them. Professional organizations, such as the National Council of Teachers of Mathematics (NCTM), the National Association for Music Education (MENC), and the International Reading Association (IRA), develop them about learning within their disciplines. Some commercially available curricula include their own outcome statements in their materials.

Many of these formal outcome statements are developed with the involvement of parents, community members, content specialists, child development experts, teachers, administrators, and other representatives of the many groups in society interested in determining what children should be learning. The outcomes often include developmental domains, but also may specify what information or facts children are expected to know.

State, federal, and local education agencies and legislative, funding, or regulatory entities adopting outcome statements may use their authority to make programs accountable for assessing and achieving those outcomes, including imposing consequences for falling short. What form this accountabil-

What's a Standard? What's a Benchmark?

At the top level in the outcomes hierarchy are statements that specify the broadest, most general expectations for what children should know and be able to do. Let's use the label *standards* for this level (see the GLOSSARY for other common labels).

Some standards are grouped by discipline, for example, mathematics, social studies, music, health, language and literacy, science, etc. State assessment guides often group standards in this way. But standards for knowledge and skills in the disciplines do not cover all aspects of development and learning, especially for young children. Many important early childhood outcomes—such as self-confidence, working with others, problem solving, decision making, self-regulation, planning, reasoning, and critical thinking—cut across all disciplines. Standards for young children's growth and development look at these habits of mind.

A standard typically is translated into at least one statement that is more specific about what children should understand or be able to do at a specific age, grade, or developmental stage with respect to that standard. From among the variety of labels given to such second-level statements, let's use *benchmarks* (see the GLOSSARY for other common labels).

Here's an example of a standard related to early literacy, followed by its benchmarks. The simpler benchmarks would apply to prekindergarten children; the others, to kindergarteners.

Standard 1

Demonstrates competence in the general skills and strategies of the reading process.

Benchmarks

1.1 Understands the basic concepts of written language.

1.2 Knows the basic conventions of reading (e.g., purpose, parts, elements, and procedures).

1.3 Knows the names of the letters of the alphabet and can identify them in any context.

1.4 Matches speech sounds with the letters or letter combinations that represent these sounds.

1.5 Converts written word into spoken word. (Bodrova et al. 2000, 7)

ity assessment is to take (e.g., standardized tests) might be specified; sometimes programs have more flexibility in what assessment they may do to meet requirements.

Local programs also develop outcome statements—if informally—when teachers, families, administrators, and other program personnel come together

---

Here is another example to show how standards and benchmarks can work together to make expectations clear:

A social studies standard "Understands basic geographic concepts" is worded to be applicable to children of any age. However, age-specific benchmarks for preschool and kindergarten children specify the "basic geographic concepts" that 4- and 5-year-olds are expected to know. Those benchmarks would be something such as "Knows geographic information about oneself (e.g., the town in which he or she lives, address, phone number)" and "Knows that maps can represent their surroundings."

Some benchmarks are worded to tell us what level of achievement is acceptable in relation to a given standard. They attempt to answer for us the question, how good is good enough? At this level of specificity, we can determine through children's words and actions not only what children know and can do but also whether that level of achievement meets the standard. For example,

For the benchmark "Engages in writing for a variety of purposes (e.g., to make lists, send messages, write stories) and in a variety of forms (e.g., sign-in sheets, journals, letters, headings on work papers)," we can collect children's messages, sign-in sheets, and journals.

For the benchmark "Describes ways the physical environment influences how people live," we can devise different ways, such as oral or written description, constructions, murals, painting, drawing, and dramatizations, for children to "describe" their understanding of the physical environment.

If the benchmarks are less specific, we may have to determine for ourselves what would be appropriate evidence. For example, for the benchmark "Understands that print carries a message," we would need to decide what evidence of "understanding" might look like. To help us do that, many curriculum and assessment guides give examples for the various standards and benchmarks that the guides address. You can use those examples to help you identify things that children in *your* group and in *your* setting do and say that are evidence of progress toward a standard or benchmark.

Adapted from Bodrova et al. 2000. Copyright © 2000 McREL.

---

to describe what they want all the children in a particular program or specific children to know and be able to do as an outcome of that program.

Teachers in programs guided by standards need to be certain that children's progress toward the expected outcomes is being assessed along the way, and that children have ample opportunity to learn what they need to know and be able to do to achieve the expected outcomes. Further, children should be assessed only on the things the program has given them the opportunity to learn. This match is important. Outcomes, curriculum, and assessment should all **align.** Once expectations for learning are agreed on, the curriculum should align with those expectations; that is, the curriculum should teach children the things they will be expected to have learned. Assessment should align with both outcomes and the curriculum, measuring what the outcomes specify and what the curriculum teaches.

Equally important is that the assessment not drive the curriculum; that is, teachers should not "teach to the test." Rather, the expectations and the curriculum should determine the assessment.

align—To line up, be consistent with, or get into position with.

When to Assess

When to do an assessment is determined by the purpose for assessment. Do we want to determine a baseline for each child's development and learning? Do we need guidance to inform our classroom planning and decision making? Must the school or center deliver information for accountability? When are family conferences?

For the classroom assessment approach that is this booklet's focus, we need to give special thought to the following times.

Before children arrive

Good assessment begins before our first day with children. We should know what the school or center expects in the way of assessment and whether there are any set times or time periods for that assessment. Find out if and when family conferences are held, because you will need to summarize information, review your records, and prepare for discussion.

Think through what information you need to collect, and develop a tentative plan for doing that. Organize needed assessment supplies. Review any required assessment forms or other tools or procedures so you are familiar with them. If you are using a state, school district, program, or commercial curriculum and assessment guide, study all the relevant materials and ask for assistance with any aspects you don't understand.

Before children enter, study their files, information from parents, and any transition information sent from previous schools or centers.

When a new group convenes

Initial assessment should occur at the beginning of the school year, when a new group comes together. This initial "sizing up" (Airasian 2000) calls for efficient procedures—simple activities and tasks for the children that not only will generate demonstrations of what they know and can do but also will leave you time to make both written and mental notes. For example,

> A teacher planning the first few days with a new group of 4-year-olds might select simple, easily supervised materials and activities so she has the freedom to observe how the children interact with one another and with the materials, how they adapt to class routines, and what they are able to do. She might make crayons, pencils, and paper available (saying, "Write your name on the paper if you know how"); simple snacks, with plenty of conversation with adults and other children; and a wide variety of books, blocks, puzzles, and the like.

Your goal is to gauge a child's or group's initial abilities, attitudes and social skills, prior knowledge and understanding, and skills and habits in relation to what the school or center emphasizes.

Don't assume anything about what children do and do not know, or can or cannot do. Assess to get started right. It is time well spent.

Day by day

Good teachers assess children day by day. Noting and recording significant milestones in children's learning and development as they occur ensures that their daily progress doesn't get overlooked.

Perhaps you take a special look at a child or two each day, using a short set of observation and question guides. Or you make a point of talking with a different child or two each day just to check in. You might record observations of two or three children each day; regularly talk with parents and other adults who work with the children; and collect children's work and take photographs of it, both on a schedule and as evidence presents itself during daily activities.

You might plan to have each child complete a writing sample during a given week or to engage the group in a science project over a period of time, noting specific knowledge and skills.

Evidence accumulates quickly if you collect it on a regular basis. Such continuous assessment is the foundation of a good classroom-based assessment effort, but it is seldom sufficient.

Periodically

Initial and final assessments that focus on important developmental domains, outcomes, and expectations show you, respectively, where you need to start with a group of children and then how well we and they did as teacher and learners.

Interim assessments can help you know how you and they are doing and whether changes need to be made. Better to check along the way than to find out at the end of your time with the children that they do not know and cannot do what is expected.

There is nothing sacred about focused assessment three times during the year; maybe four times or five times is more appropriate for you, a particular group of children, or one or more important learning goals. Whatever the number, if you plan periodic assessments for a time shortly before family conferences you will have current, significant information to share. If you do day-by-day assessment conscientiously, you may have enough information already and may need only to summarize it rather than do a separate interim assessment.

Periodic assessments help us to monitor progress in different domains or toward specific outcomes and expectations.

Before and after a project, theme, or curriculum emphasis

Occasionally even regular assessment and day-to-day interaction with children don't give us sufficient information for classroom planning and decision making.

Before you make final plans for any sustained unit, project, or emphasis, assess the children's attitudes, any prerequisite knowledge or skills, and their current understanding of concepts related to what they are supposed to be learning in the unit. You may find that some of the children have already mastered the skills and content you had been planning to include, and that other children need to start at a more basic level than you had proposed to begin with. Don't assume; check to find out.

Then after a curriculum unit or emphasis, assess to see what individual children have mastered and what they may need continuing help with.

As needed to address a problem or concern

We need to take a closer look at a child or a group when there is a specific problem or concern. Is there a health problem? Something going on at home? An issue of context or environment? A behavior that does not develop or change at the expected rate? Collect information before you start seeking solutions. For example,

> Circle time is a disaster day after day, so we collect data on what is actually going on: When do the children stop paying attention? Is it one child or most of the children? Are there external distractions? Are children restless because they smell and hear lunch being prepared?

> At mid-year a 4-year-old writes her name the same way she did on the first day of school. She jabs at the paper, holds the pencil or marker in a fist, and does not form any letters. Does this fit developmental expectations?

After you have identified the specific problem or concern, you may be able to address it through classroom instruction. In other cases, you may want to have a conference about a particular child with parents or specialists. Make sure you are prepared for the conference with up-to-date, relevant information.

Other time considerations

Be sensitive to the possible impact that time-related factors—such as time of day, distractions such as seasonal holidays and impending special events, or being rushed—can have on children's ability to perform.

For example, many young children (adults too) are not at their best right after lunch. Assessing when there is lots of holiday hoopla in the air also may give a misleading picture of distracted children's learning and development.

Gathering Information about Children

Obviously we cannot look into children's heads to see directly what each of them knows and is able to do. Instead, we have only the things children say and do as indications of their development and learning. So we assess those things. And we must assess them sufficiently to be confident that our picture of the children is trustworthy.

How much assessment information is sufficient will vary depending on our purpose. To make an everyday classroom decision—the choice of a particular book, for example—a teacher needs only a general idea of "where children are." She can change direction easily if the book she chooses is over the children's heads.

By contrast, to make an important decision about children and their education, we should assess using *multiple measures*—meaning that information should be gathered from different sources, at different times, in different settings or contexts, using different recording methods. Our basic definition of assessment captures that need: "Assessment is the process of *gathering information about children from several forms of evidence,* then organizing and interpreting that information."

This step (sometimes called *documenting*) of systematically gathering information about what children say and do has two parts. The first part is choosing a method or approach in order to *find out*. The second is choosing a format or method or tool to *make a record* of what we find.

Find out

There are five basic ways of gathering information about children to document their development and learning. A full discussion of each way is beyond the scope of this booklet. Each has advantages and challenges; each is suited to some purposes and not others; each has its own tools, proponents, and critics. For more information about them, the FOR MORE INFORMATION section points to some excellent sources.

Assessment that combines the first *three* ways—observing systematically, studying work products, and eliciting responses—is the most widely used and accepted approach for determining what young children know and can do.

Observe children systematically

This kind of observation is not the same as the casual kind that we might do watching children at play in the park.

To observe systematically, we watch and listen attentively as children work, play, and live together. We note their facial expressions, tone of voice, what they say and how they say it, how they move, and how they go about completing tasks and whether they complete them. We observe children alone; we observe them as members of a group. We observe them in spontaneous activities and in tasks or situations we have arranged.

As observers, we cannot take in everything, so we focus: on certain children, certain situations, or certain aspects of a child's development and learning, depending on what we need to find out. At the same time, our lens must be transparent. We must describe exactly what a child says or does, not jump to conclusions about what we think it might mean. "Kimberly hit Stevie when he reached for her blocks" is an observation; "Kimberly is really aggressive" is not.

Study children's work products

During the course of a day, children produce drawings, paintings, writings, computer printouts, graphs, field notes (in science), constructions, dramatizations, oral presentations. We call all of these rich sources of information children's **work products.** They reveal a child's individual "style" and development as they give vivid evidence of what a child knows and can do. Children's work products can document individual as well as group experiences.

Two big pluses for busy teachers are that work products can be put aside to be studied later, away from the bustle of the classroom, and they can be saved as evidence of children's learning.

> **work product**—A tangible item from children's work and play that gives evidence of their learning or development.

Elicit responses from children

We get clues to children's development and learning when we ask children questions, make requests, give directions, lead discussions, assign tasks, set up equipment in a particular way, provide particular materials, and conduct short conferences and interviews. First and second grade teachers may be able to use short written assignments and tests.

How we frame our interaction with the child or the child's interaction with materials determines what *type of response* we will get. Our aim should

---

Think Before You Ask—Selected vs. Constructed Responses

We elicit a *selected response* when we have children choose from among a limited range of options. For example, we might ask a child to "point to the red box" when we show him a red, a yellow, and a blue box.

We elicit a *constructed response* when we have children recall, com-bine, and apply their knowledge and skills in a response they build from scratch. For example, we might ask the child to name all the things she knows that are red. Often a constructed response generates richer, more complex information for interpretation.

always be to get children to respond in ways that both advance their learning and help us find out what the children have and have not learned. This aim is a fundamental element of authentic performance assessment.

Note how children respond to your assistance during instruction

Sometimes important assessment information is revealed as we are teaching. Keep track of your hints, prompts, and helps that assisted particular children to learn. For example, during a first grade journal writing activity, the teacher found that some children needed only an alphabet chart to start writing; others needed to look at the "word wall"; still others needed help brainstorming ideas.

Seek information from other adults

Insight from family members, fellow teachers, assistants, specialists, and support staff can enlarge and deepen our understanding of the children we work with. Ask for their perspectives. Look in the child's file.

Parents and other family members have known their child longer and more intimately than anyone else, and they may see aspects of that child not revealed at school. In addition, family members are our primary window into a child's home culture and any home-school differences. Fellow teachers and classroom assistants who work with the children in our group may have experiences and insights to add, as will speech and language specialists or others who work with specific children individually.

Make a record

The second part of documenting is making a record of what we find. We make records for several reasons. No teacher can remember everything she might like to about even one child, let alone 15 or more children. Records remind us as we plan, report to parents, confer with children, or collaborate with colleagues. When someone asks, "How do you know that?" or "What evidence do you have?" we should be able to turn to our **documentation.**

> **documentation**—A record made of evidence of what a child or group of children have done or accomplished.

Often teachers devise their own ways of recording, such as creating a form or checklist tailored to their unique needs. Sometimes ready-to-use materials are available; for example, in state, district, and commercial assessment guides.

Most ways of recording that teachers typically use fit into one of four types: records that describe, those that count/tally, those that rate/rank, and those that are made by the children themselves. Each type of record has advantages and disadvantages that may or may not make it a good choice for your assessment purpose.

Records that describe

Narrative records are descriptions of a child, situation, or event that are written by you or other adults in your classroom. They will vary in length and in amount of detail. One common type is an *anecdotal* record, in which the teacher records a short description of an incident involving one or several children. Here are two examples of anecdotal records:

> 1/22/03—Anjoulie came to school before everyone else. Announced, "I came firster 'n everybody." Went immediately to book area, picked out the three new books, and sat on the floor to look at them.

> 3/13/03—Enlisting the aid of Josh and Omar, Dreshawn took charge of returning all the blocks to their correct places on the shelves. Said, "We're gonna do it ourselves." When the other boys put blocks in the wrong places, D. changed them. "No, they go here." "No, this way." Josh and Omar left before finishing. D. put the rest of the blocks away by himself.

Another narrative type is short *jottings*, or informative phrases that can add explanation to other kinds of records. For example, in the margin of a child's work product or a participation chart, you might jot down:

> Named each object in his drawing.

> Siddeth watched. Did not join in.

Your *diagrams, sketches,* and *photographs* are "visual jottings" and are a quick way to preserve important details that would otherwise require elaborate written descriptions. Properly annotated (with the child's name, date, setting or context of the work, comments about its significance, and other relevant

information), such records are a rich source of evidence of children's learning and development. For example, a photograph of a complicated pattern a child made with cubes can demonstrate that child's recognition of and ability to duplicate and extend patterns. Figure 1 [located at the end of this section] provides an example of an annotated photograph.

A *concept map* can document a group's understanding of a specific topic, problem, or idea at a given point in time. Such a record helps identify what various children do and do not understand about the relationships among concepts and what they do or do not know about a topic. Concept maps can take a variety of forms, including lists and webs. Figure 2 provides an example.

Audiotapes and *videotapes* can document transient work products and events. Children's discussions, presentations, exhibits, displays, dramatizations, reading aloud, and oral reporting (e.g., telling about their investigation of a science project) all lend themselves to these kinds of records. While you tape, focus on that element of the children's learning and development that is important to preserve because too much material can be overwhelming to transcribe or analyze later.

Records that count or tally

These records capture information about the occurrence (or *frequency*) of a particular behavior or event. How long a child keeps up a particular behavior (its *duration*) can also be recorded.

Checklists are one of the most widely used recording methods because they are time efficient and can be constructed to capture information on almost anything having to do with children's development and learning. Seemingly endless variations on what to check for and how to mark are possible. Checklists can display a lot of information about an individual child or a smaller amount of information about a group of children. Information can be captured over time, so you do not have to assess everything or every child all at once. Designing the checklist to capture information from several assessments over time will document children's progress. Figure 3 shows a checklist.

Participation charts can be constructed to show not only which children participated in a given activity, for how long, and how often but also the

Looking at the Children as a Group

Teachers plan for individual children, but they also plan for the class as a whole. What experiences would be most beneficial in the coming weeks and months? What changes in the environment should be made? To help address such questions, recording methods that show where the entire group of children stands in relation to a particular goal or developmental accomplishment are efficient. They give you a class profile that shows the range of knowledge and skills in the group—that is, what the most knowledgeable and the least knowledgeable children know, what the most and least proficient can do.

The checklist shown in Figure 3 is an example of such a record. Participation charts can also be constructed to record evidence about a whole group.

Often such assessments reveal groupings or clusters of children who could benefit from similar activities targeting their shared needs. Records that profile all the children are very useful in curriculum planning.

quality of a child's participation. For example, the length of time a child stays focused on an activity provides evidence of her self-regulation and ability to focus attention—skills underlying learning. Charts also can be designed to be filled in by the children themselves. See Figure 4 for a participation chart.

Teachers can use participation charts to study their own behavior, too. Collect the information yourself, or perhaps ask another adult to observe you in action. For example, does the evidence show that you tend to spend disproportionate time with some children or in some areas of the room?

In a *frequency count,* you make a tally mark each time a behavior occurs, documenting the number of occurrences over a defined period. For example, a teacher seeking to foster a rather nonverbal child's language development and use might begin by tallying his verbalizations in different classroom centers and contexts to assess which situations are most likely to promote his expressive language.

Records that rate or rank

These records document our judgments, conclusions, and evaluations of what a child knows and can do by assigning a child's performance a rank or standing on a continuum. The continuum may be based on children's typical development or on a predetermined standard.

Records that rate or rank can document broad judgments or can focus on fine distinctions in the quality of a child's performance. They are often used to document complex behavior such as writing or problem solving. Ratings and rankings should be based on solid evidence, not our impressions or opinions.

With a *rating scale,* we assign the child a rank or rating along a scale (see Figure 5 for an example). In school most of us were graded on a rating scale of A–F. Here are some other widely used rating scales:

Advanced, Proficient, Partially proficient, Needs development

Needs development, Developing, Mastered

Never, Sometimes, Usually, Always

A *rubric* or *scoring guide* provides clear criteria, rules, guidelines, or descriptions by which the child's performance is judged (see Figure 6 for an example of a rubric). Frequently the rubric specifies the conditions under which a child's achievement is to be judged as acceptable—e.g., which or how many criteria must be met or the quality of performance.

Records made by children

Children's *work products* (e.g., their drawings, constructions, oral presentations) are a type of record that children make themselves. Such records are made more meaningful when they include the children's oral comments about their work and your brief description of the context in which the work products were produced.

The same work product can document more than one aspect of a child's development and learning. For example, a kindergartener's journal entry can be used to document the child's developing knowledge of print as well as her interests.

Choose a procedure

Sometimes the kind of assessment to use is mandated. Sometimes we have more flexibility to create or choose our own, and matching procedure to purpose is always fundamental. Determining the appropriate assessment to use involves some careful thought. Here are some considerations to keep in mind.

What is being assessed? A specific behavior or understanding—for example, walking a 6-inch balance beam or identifying letters by name—is discrete enough to record on a checklist. Broad outcome areas—for example, language development, self-regulation, cooperation, and attitudes toward reading or mathematics—call for a more descriptive method (a narrative, for example) or a method that captures the behavior's complexity (maybe a rubric).

How much detail is needed? Some methods capture rich, detailed information, and others do not. To document children's progress in understanding story structure, for example, a teacher can gather and examine each child's dictated stories and writing samples, and so on.

What is practical? Some records require a lot of classroom time and attention, and teachers' time is finite. Checklists, participation charts, frequency counts, and short anecdotal records, as well as collecting children's work products, are easily worked into classroom routines and can provide much useful information.

Do you need information on one child or on the group? Some ways of recording information—group checklists and participation charts, for example—can display an entire group's standing in relation to a desired result. This perspective enables a teacher to think about how to help the entire group advance their learning.

Are you monitoring progress over time? If you want to compare a child's behavior over time, use the same type of record and capture the same level of detail each time you assess, so your assessments are comparable. In addition, the way you collect information and the context used should be similar.

What is your assessment experience and understanding at this time? Beginning teachers should give themselves time and opportunity to learn by using simple recording techniques at first. Teachers experienced in assessment and in classroom management may be ready to use more demanding recording schemes.

Figure 1. Annotated photograph

Portfolio Entry Form

Child Nate Curtis   Date 2/11/02 —   Observer E.B.

Context/Setting: Manipulatives; choice time

Comments/Significance:

Extend — these work. Work on words for explanation

Nate worked with the Cuisenaire rods the entire choice time (45 min). Persuaded Angie & Cody, the other 2 children working with C. rods, to let him use all the orange rods. Carefully lined up rods; created AB pattern for most of length. Some trial & error in locating the correct length of shorter rods to equal the orange (10) rod, but not mistakes in final product. Demonstrates knowledge of alternating pattern, grasp of "equal in length," & excellent muscle control for 4. Unable to explain why the large number of orange rods on the right, & their absence on the left; unable to articulate pattern even though he had made it. Maintained focus on this self-chosen task. Not seen — social skills of obtaining willing cooperation from peers.

Figure 2. Concept map

Developed during a discussion between a group of 3- and 4-year-olds and their teacher, this concept map shows the children's understandings about "school."

Most of these preschoolers readily gave accurate responses—some in sentences—to what they do and who they see in school. They recognized and responded to all the categories being considered. One child's responses ("marker," "We leaf") were clearly off the mark, alerting the teacher to a possible concern with that child's language and conceptual ability.

Fewer children responded to how they feel at school and what they are learning. If expanding children's understanding of and ability to talk about those more abstract topics is a goal, this quick assessment indicates that the children may need more help.

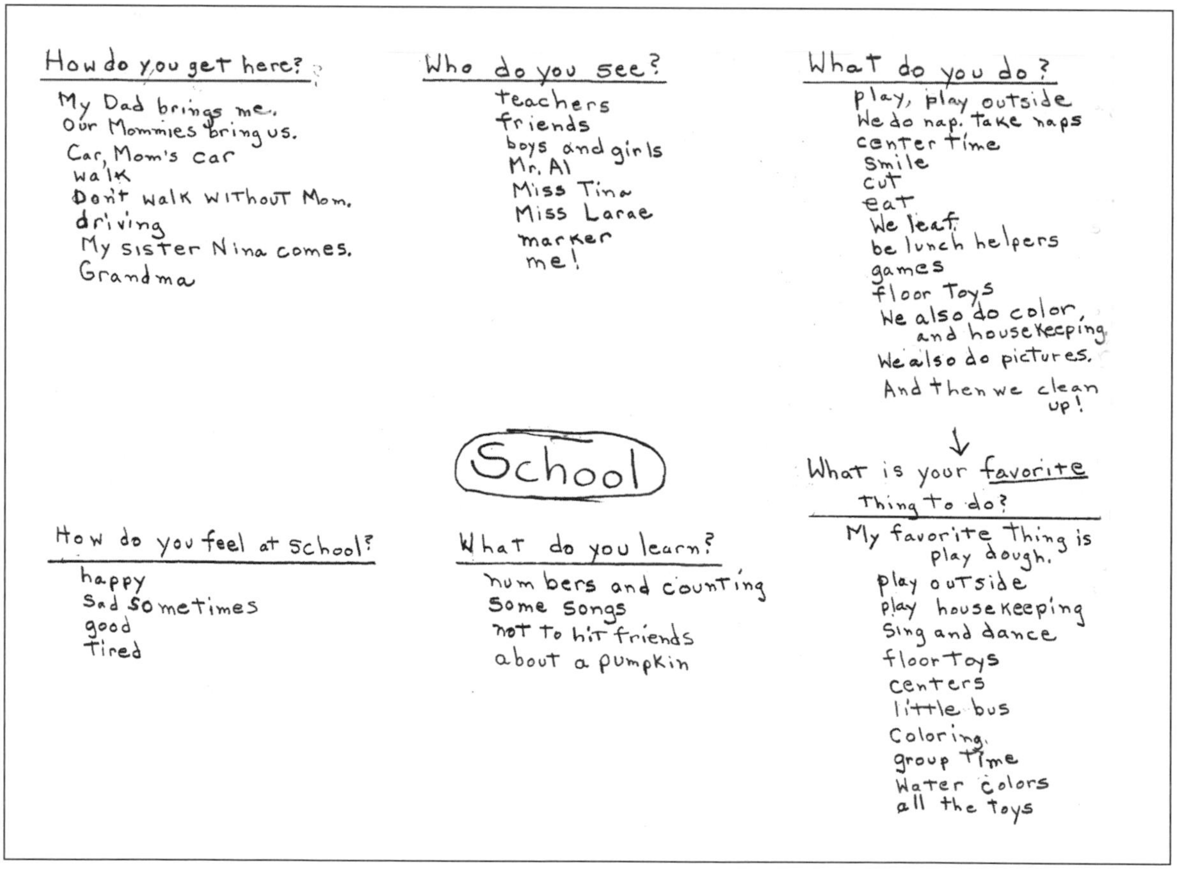

How do you get here?
My Dad brings me.
Our Mommies bring us.
Car, Mom's car
walk
Don't walk without Mom.
driving
My sister Nina comes.
Grandma

Who do you see?
teachers
friends
boys and girls
Mr. Al
Miss Tina
Miss Larae
marker
me!

What do you do?
play, play outside
We do nap. take naps
center time
Smile
cut
eat
We leaf.
be lunch helpers
games
floor Toys
We also do color,
    and housekeeping
We also do pictures.
And then we clean
    up!

(School)

What is your favorite Thing to do?
My favorite Thing is
    play dough.
play outside
play housekeeping
Sing and dance
floor Toys
centers
little bus
Coloring.
group time
Water colors
all the Toys

How do you feel at school?
happy
Sad sometimes
good
Tired

What do you learn?
numbers and counting
Some Songs
not to hit friends
about a pumpkin

Figure 3. Checklist for assessing a group of children on their literacy skills

Date: _____ Legend	Identifies facts.	Uses the information to retell what has been read in own words.	Interprets symbols.	Handles books appropriately.	Identifies some print conventions.	Letter	Word	Capital Letter	Period	Identifies some book conventions.	Front cover	Title	Author	Illustrator	Title page	Spine	Demonstrates directionality and return sweep.	Demonstrates matching one spoken word with one written word.
✔ Exhibits behavior regularly + Making progress ✳ Has not yet exhibited the behavior																		
Names																		

From Rigby KinderStarters. Reprinted with permission of Harcourt Achieve.

Figure 4. Participation chart for a small group discussion

Make a tally mark for each response or request.	Asks question; Makes Request	Responds to Question / Request	Volunteers Information / Comment	Irrelevant Action or Comment
Observer **Damien T.** (volunteer) — Date **04/15/04** Group **AM Kindergarten**				
Teacher - Vialfondo, Tila				
Amanda, T.				
Amned, S.				
Emily, L.				
Farid, H.				
Ryan A.				
Sarah, W.				

Figure 5. Rating scale

Children are rated on their retelling of a story, as evidence of their skills and understandings in 12 literacy-related areas.

Retelling	None	Low Degree	Moderate Degree	High Degree
1. Includes information directly stated in text.		⊬		
2. Includes information inferred directly or indirectly from the text.			⊬	
3. Includes what is important to remember from the text.			⊬	
4. Provides relevant content and concepts.			⊬	
5. Indicates reader's attempt to connect background knowledge to text information.		⊬		
6. Indicates reader's attempt to make summary statements or generalizations based on text that can be applied to the real world.			⊬	
7. Indicates highly individualistic and creative impressions of or reactions to the text.			⊬	
8. Indicates the reader's affective involvement with the text.		⊬		
9. Demonstrates appropriate use of language (vocabulary, sentence structure, language conventions).			⊬	
10. Indicates reader's ability to organize or compose the retelling.			⊬	
11. Demonstrates the reader's sense of audience or purpose.		⊬		
12. Indicates the reader's control of the mechanics of speaking or writing.		⊬		

From Morrow, L. 1988. Retelling stories as a diagnostic tool. In S.M. Glazer, L.W. Searfoss, & L.M. Gentile, eds., *Reexamining Reading Diagnosis: New Trends and Procedures*, 128–49. Newark, DE: International Reading Association. Reprinted with permission of Lesley M. Morrow and the International Reading Association. All rights reserved.

Figure 6. A rubric for scoring "Expresses Ideas Clearly"

A. *Expresses ideas clearly*

4   Clearly and effectively communicates the main idea or theme and provides support that contains rich, vivid, and powerful detail.

3   Clearly communicates the main idea or theme and provides suitable support and detail.

2   Communicates important information but not a clear theme or overall structure.

1   Communicates information as isolated pieces in a random fashion.

Reprinted from R.J. Marzano, D. Pickering, & J. McTighe, *Assessing Student Outcomes: Performance Assessment Using the Dimensions of Learning Model.* Alexandria, VA: Association for Supervision and Curriculum Development, 1993, 85. Copyright © 1993 McREL. Reprinted by permission.

Looking at the Information You Gathered

The second part of our basic definition of assessment describes this next stage in the assessment cycle: "Assessment is the process of gathering information about children from several forms of evidence, then *organizing and interpreting that information.*"

Compiling and summarizing

What do you do with all those anecdotal records, rubrics, checklists, work products, photographs, and notes from discussions with parents that you have filed every day (. . . well, maybe every week or so) over several weeks or months of collecting and recording evidence about each child? Perhaps parent meetings are coming up, interim progress reports are due, or you need guidance for curriculum planning in important content areas.

A systematic organizational process will help you compile and summarize the large amount of information, as the first step toward deciding what the information tells you about the children's development and learning. One method for organizing information is to use a *portfolio* approach. Another method is to create a summary of compiled information.

What Is a Portfolio?

A portfolio is a purposeful collection of evidence of a child's learning, collected over time, that demonstrates a child's efforts, progress, or achievement. Physically a portfolio might be a folder, box, or drawer devoted to the collection. It is not itself an assessment; it is a way of storing and displaying evidence from various types of assessments.

A child's portfolio might contain work samples of all kinds, photographs and accompanying explanations of significant constructions and activities, writing samples (from scribbles to stories), interviews, lists of books read, and other artifacts of learning. It might also contain any number of records about the child, such as rating scales, anecdotal records, and checklists.

In *portfolio assessment*, there is a systematic process for determining what goes in the portfolio, when and by whom (adult or child) a piece of evidence is collected, and how it is evaluated. Maybe that process dictates that portfolios contain similar items for all children, or that they reflect children's individual interests and strengths.

Most assessment guides provide summary information sheets that you can use. Both individual child and group summary sheets have important uses. Figures 7 and 8 [located at the end of this section] show examples of different approaches to compiling comprehensive information about an individual child. Figure 9 is a summary sheet profiling the progress of an entire class in areas of learning valued in that program. It is easy to see how useful class summaries are in planning for the group.

Many school districts and large early childhood programs provide their teachers with summary sheets, often keyed to their programs' expected outcomes and tied to progress reports for parents. Other programs develop their own sheets of easily constructed grids and forms specific to that individual program's goals. Some early childhood programs use computer software to help compile, organize, and summarize collected information. Several commercial curriculum and assessment guides accompany their materials with such software.

However, the most critical thing that happens in summarizing is that we study and reflect on the possible meaning of the evidence we have so diligently collected. As we fit the pieces of evidence into a coherent whole, we develop a better understanding of each child and of the group. Summaries are useful for parents and administrators, but the person who learns the most from a summary is the teacher who compiles it!

Interpreting

In this step, we interpret the objective information we compiled with sensitivity, using our knowledge of children. We consider the evidence we have systematically collected, recorded, and summarized, using our best professional judgment and the understanding and insight that come from daily interactions with children. These challenges are part of what makes interpretation a high-level professional activity of teachers.

The guidelines that follow will help you in deciding what the assessment information you have gathered might—and might *not*—mean.

Ensure the adequacy of the information

Your interpretation can be only as sound as the assessments you used, and it is most likely to be trustworthy when based on evidence from different sources, methods, and contexts. Work from recorded information, not memory. Draw your inferences from the patterns you see in your compilations and summaries of the evidence, not from bits of information in isolation.

Compare evidence with expectations

It is not very useful to document simply that a child can do two out of five motor activities on a skills checklist or understands seven out of ten of the "concepts of print." When it is time to interpret our assessment results, we need some frame of reference to help us determine what those results mean in terms of that child's learning. Is seven "good enough," or does the child's performance still need to improve?

If the outcome statements (e.g., standards or benchmarks) you are working with are specific enough, you can often make a direct comparison and determine what a child knows and can do in relation to those expected outcomes. Here's an example:

> Part of the assessment information you have collected relates to important science objectives in the school's curriculum guide. One of these objectives is that children "Use attributes and functions of objects to *group* those that are alike."

> From a variety of evidence you have collected—observations of children working on their own; records of what children have done or said in interaction with adults and other children as they worked with materials they could group; photographs, drawings, and graphs that demonstrate their understanding of grouping—you can make a trustworthy determination of what the children have learned and what remains to be learned in relation to the expected outcome.

> Some of the children may be able to group objects on observable attributes but not on functions; some may be able to do both.

> From this information you can develop activities to keep all the children progressing toward this objective that identifies skills and understanding basic to all learning.

Note that in our example, the focus was on what each child had learned in relation to a standard (*criterion-referencing*), not whether the child was average, above average, or below average compared with what the other children knew (*norm-referencing*). This is an important distinction to make between two approaches to understanding what assessment results mean.

That said, meeting a standard is not the sum total of what you need to consider with respect to a child's development and learning. For example, often a child can and should go far beyond the skills and understandings called for in the benchmarks for a standard. You will want to think about what else that child can explore and how you can encourage further learning.

Compare evidence with a developmental continuum

Information you collect about what children know and can do takes on additional meaning when you look at that information in the context of a *developmental continuum*. Such a continuum describes the typical sequence of

Norm-Referencing vs. Criterion-Referencing

It is not the assessment tasks or items that distinguish an assessment as *norm-referenced* or *criterion-referenced*. Instead, the distinctive element is the comparison. Here is an example that may feel familiar from your own school experiences:

> Matt and Justin are second-graders in different classrooms. Each takes the same math test. Matt's teacher says that only the top five scores in the class will earn an A. Because his test score will be compared against his classmates' scores, Matt's math assessment is *norm-referenced*. In Justin's classroom, his teacher says that a score of at least 9 out of a possible 10 points will earn an A. Because each student's score in Justin's classroom is looked at independent of the other students' scores, his math assessment is *criterion-referenced*.

In norm-referencing, the comparison is with children who have taken the same assessment—the *norming group*. The norming group could be a national sample, the child's own classmates (as in Matt's case above), or anything in between. In assessing growth and development, our norming group might be "typically developing children"—a profile developed from the study of many human children over many years. A height screening, for example, is a comparison with children's typical height at that age, and therefore is a norm-referenced assessment. Results on a norm-referenced assessment are reported in terms such as whether a child scored above or below the average (or *mean*), or performed as well or better than a given portion of the norming group (*percentile*).

Standardized achievement tests typically are norm-referenced; for example, the Iowa Tests of Basic Skills, the Metropolitan Achievement Tests, and the California Achievement Tests. Norm-referenced assessment can indicate the relative standing of schools, districts, and states, as well as their standing relative to a national sample. For example, policymakers might want to know whether students in schools receiving low funding do as well on the tests as students from affluent schools do. Intelligence tests such as the Stanford-Binet and the Weschler Intelligence Scale for Children (WISC) and standardized screening tests such as the Early Screening Inventory and the Developmental Indicators for the Assessment of Learning-Revised (DIAL-R) are also norm-referenced.

In the classroom, a teacher's first impulse may be to compare children with other children in a group. But if only a few children are way behind the rest, do we conclude that everything is okay? Even if the entire group perform similarly, are they all behind or ahead of where they should be? To know that, we need to compare each child's performance with curriculum expectations—as in the grouping example (on the previous page). In other words, has each child acquired the knowledge or skill identified in our *criterion* (i.e., in our standard, benchmark, objective) as being important? Information from criterion-referenced assessments is directly useful in deciding what children have yet to learn.

Most assessments aligned with standards, whether developed by commercial publishers or education systems, are criterion-referenced.

child development and learning. Sometimes the continuum identifies the steps of the sequence as being associated with certain ages, stages, or grade levels, with the caution that all children must not be expected to progress at the same rate or reach a particular step at the same time. A continuum provides a starting framework for thinking about what range of things to work on with a group of children at a particular age or grade.

By comparing information about a particular child with the developmental continuum, you can approximate where in development that child is now, which milestones and understandings the child has mastered to reach that point, and which should occur later if the child gets appropriate learning experiences and opportunities. For example, young children differ dramatically in their ability to hold and use writing and drawing instruments, an essential skill even in today's mouse-and-keyboard world. Some children's first encounter with pencils, pens, crayons, and markers comes in kindergarten; for others it comes much earlier. Some children gain fine muscle control early; others struggle for years. But there is a predictable sequence in how children's abilities typically develop, as shown in Figure 10. The examples of children's work show points in this developmental sequence.

Referring to the continuum informs our interpretation of the evidence we have gathered (and may guide our next steps). Do the children's abilities fall in a range appropriate for their age and developmental level? If not, what might be the reasons? What additional evidence might add to our understanding?

Compare performances at two or more points in time

We can draw conclusions about what progress a child has made if we have collected evidence over time in such a way that the evidence is comparable. One way to ensure comparability is to use the same assessment procedures each time; that is, to use a *standardized* approach. For example, you might compare writing samples with previous writing samples that used the same tools and paper; or compare physical dexterity on tasks that used the same equipment, setup, and directions.

Whether the child is making *enough* progress would be a separate comparison of performance with expectations or typical development.

What "Standardized" Assessment Is and Isn't

Standardized is not—or should not be—a dirty word in early childhood assessment. We do assessment that is standardized when we do our best to be consistent and uniform, or *standard*, in our methods so results can be compared. If we assess different children for the same skill or understanding, or the same child over time, we give the same instructions, allow the same amount of time, provide the same materials, look for the same behavior, follow the same steps, record information on the same form. We can develop and use standard procedures for making certain kinds of observations, for collecting children's work products, and for eliciting their responses. Standardization saves time, as well as increases the reliability and fairness of our assessments.

The photos below show a simple, standard cutting task that a teacher had children do over a period of several days. Provided with the same kind of paper and scissors, each child was to snip on the short lines, cut on the line across the paper, and cut on the curved line to produce the semicircle. The two examples show the range in abilities of the group.

As part of such an assessment it would be important to observe the children while they were cutting, to see how each held the scissors and paper. The child whose work is shown on the left could benefit from some help learning to use scissors.

Standardized assessment can also refer to something more elaborate and structured in which procedures and instruments are specified, teachers are trained in how to use them, and the assessments are expected to be consistent and comparable across classrooms, schools, and centers. The Work Sampling System (Meisels et al. 2001) is one example. The system consists of three standard components—a developmental checklist, a portfolio of children's work, and summary reports of children's progress. The processes that teachers are taught in order to gather and interpret the basic information in the classroom are also standardized.

The most standardized assessment is the *standardized test*. Specially constructed according to a set of testing standards (see AERA/APA/NCME 1999), a standardized test requires a trained examiner to administer it and interpret its scores. Standardized tests often are used for accountability purposes and in the screening and diagnosis of special needs.

Standardized testing of young children is controversial. NAEYC's (2003) position statement *Early Childhood Curriculum, Assessment, and Program Evaluation* offers guidance in using the results of standardized tests and how to safeguard young children.

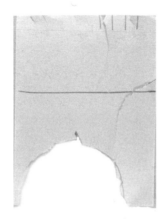
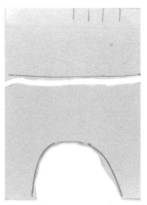

Recognize that a child's level of functioning varies

A child's performance on any one assessment should be seen as an indicator of that child's *range* of functioning (skills, understandings, development), rather than as an indicator of "true" performance. In fact, it is not necessary—and usually is not possible—to identify a child's level of functioning precisely.

Thinking in terms of a range makes sense in view of the difficulty in assessing young children and the variable nature of their development and learning. What any young child seems to know and be able to do as measured by a specific assessment at a specific time also significantly depends on a number of factors, including the extent to which you helped the child with the assessment, whether the child is just beginning to learn or has achieved mastery, and possible errors in measurement.

Consider the context

Because young children behave differently in different contexts, some assessment information makes sense only if you consider the time, setting, environmental influences, available materials, people involved, and possible home and community influences. For example, looking at the context, we should suspect environmental circumstances are challenging this child's ability to focus attention on the learning tasks at hand:

> Levon is an active, friendly first-grader whose performance has begun to deteriorate. Since her teacher rearranged the classroom, sometimes Levon does not finish a task, rushes through, or doesn't follow directions, especially in the work period that follows recess. Levon now faces the classroom's open doorway into a busy hall. She shares the table with her two best friends. And she must turn sideways in her chair to see the whiteboard and the teacher.

In addition, factors having to do with the adult doing the assessment—for example, his or her familiarity to the child and level of assessment skills—make an enormous difference in a young child's performance in one-on-one assessment situations.

Seek the insights of others

Some teachers find that discussion with other teachers is one of their most valuable tools for trying to figure out what the wealth of assessment information means. This interaction may be especially valuable if you are a newcomer to assessment and you have access to colleagues with more experience.

Talking with children's families can also give teachers insights that are very useful in interpreting various kinds of assessment evidence. Family members may describe things the child does at home, for example, that you have not observed in the classroom or found in other assessments. This information can alert you to go back and try other ways to tap the child's knowledge and skills.

Interpret cautiously, conclude tentatively, and recheck

Interpreting the assessment you do for immediate classroom use does not require as many safeguards as interpreting information that may be reported to parents, next year's teacher, or an outside agency. In the classroom, if you see you have misjudged, you can immediately adjust. But if you are assessing for the purpose of accountability or in decisions such as placement or referral, the consequences of a hasty or mistaken interpretation can be serious.

Review your assessment's reliability and validity. Look for bias. Consider the challenges unique to the assessment of young children such as their uneven development, sensitivity to context, and all the rest. Assess again later; assess in another way.

Always consider several possible interpretations of the information. Among those possibilities, consider whether you are being less than objective in your interpretation. For example, perhaps we have blamed children for their rowdy behavior at transitions, until a more objective look reveals that we are part of the problem by hurrying the children to get ready for the next activity.

Learning about children and learning from children as we assess them can yield insights into ourselves that help us to grow as teachers and as people. Looking beneath the labels we may so readily apply enables us to "see" youngsters in a different light and respond to them in more appropriate ways.

This challenge, for teachers to continually self-monitor and self-correct, is another reason why insightful, on-target interpretation is such a high-level professional activity.

Figure 7. A summary sheet on an individual child

This one-page *Child Progress and Planning Report*, by Teaching Strategies, is a form for a narrative record, designed as a report for the child's parents as well as a summary sheet.

THE **CREATIVE CURRICULUM®**
FOR PRESCHOOL

Child Progress and Planning Report

Child's Name:_____   Date:_____

Teacher(s):_____   Family Member(s):_____

Summary of Developmental Progress:

SOCIAL/EMOTIONAL	COGNITIVE
Sense of Self; Responsibility for Self and Others; Prosocial Behavior	Learning and Problem Solving; Logical Thinking; Representation and Symbolic Thinking

PHYSICAL	LANGUAGE
Gross Motor; Fine Motor	Listening and Speaking; Reading and Writing

FAMILY COMMENTS AND OBSERVATIONS:	NEXT STEPS AT SCHOOL AND AT HOME:

Teacher(s) Signature:_____   Family Member(s) Signature:_____

Reprinted with permission from Dodge, D.T., Colker, L.J., & Heroman, C., *The Creative Curriculum® Developmental Continuum Assessment Toolkit for Ages 3-5*, Child Progress and Planning Report. © 2001 Teaching Strategies, Inc., Washington, DC, www.TeachingStrategies.com.

Figure 8. A summary sheet on an individual child

This page is part of the *Work Sampling System Kindergarten Developmental Checklist, 4th ed.*, used to profile an individual child's performance on the system's seven "major domains of learning." Each domain ("Personal and Social Development" etc.) is broken into "functional components" ("Self concept" etc.) designating the domain's content emphasis. "Performance indicators" ("Demonstrates self-confidence" etc.) in each component state the skills, behavior, attitudes, and accomplishments that teachers have taught and assessed. A later blank page gives the teacher space for recording additional information about the child.

Basics of Assessment

Figure 9. A summary sheet on a group

This *Class Summary Form* is part of High/Scope's observational assessment tool the *Preschool Child Observation Record (COR), 2d ed.* The form summarizes COR results for a whole group for up to three assessments.

Class Summary

In the columns below, enter the Category Averages and COR Total scores for each child in the group from his or her Child Information and Developmental Summary form. To obtain Class Averages in each Category, add the Category Averages in each column and divide the result by the number of children in your class. To obtain Class Growth in each category from Time 1 to Time 2, subtract the Time 1 Class Average from the Time 2 Class Average. To determine percentage growth, divide the Time 2 Class Average by the Time 1 Class Average, and then subtract 1 (e.g., if your result is .243, this indicates 24% growth). To calculate growth from Time 2 to Time 3 or from Time 1 to Time 3, follow the same steps.

Class: _____
Name: _____
Teacher: _____

Scoring Period:
Time 1 ___/___/___ to ___/___/___
Time 2 ___/___/___ to ___/___/___
Time 3 ___/___/___ to ___/___/___

	Initiative			Social Relations			Creative Representation			Movement & Music			Language & Literacy			Mathematics & Science			COR Total		
	Time 1	Time 2	Time 3	Time 1	Time 2	Time 3	Time 1	Time 2	Time 3	Time 1	Time 2	Time 3	Time 1	Time 2	Time 3	Time 1	Time 2	Time 3	Time 1	Time 2	Time 3
1																					
2																					
3																					
4																					
5																					
6																					
7																					
8																					
9																					
10																					
11																					
12																					
13																					
14																					
15																					
16																					
17																					
18																					
19																					
20																					
21																					
22																					
23																					
24																					
25																					
Category Totals																					
Class Category Average																					
Class Growth: Time 2 – Time 1																					
Class Growth: Time 3 – Time 2																					
Class Growth: Time 3 – Time 1																					

P1214
Copyright © 2003 High/Scope Educational Research Foundation
ISBN 1-57379-192-X

Copyright © 2003 High/Scope Educational Research Foundation.

Figure 10. A developmental continuum for "use of writing tools," and samples of various children's work

Most children:

• Grasp writing implements with whole hand or fist; jab at paper; make scribbles with movement of whole arm; copy vertical and horizontal lines. (2–3 yrs.)

• Try a three-point grasp but position on instrument inconsistent; copy a cross and a circle; scribble with spots of intense color; use horizontal and vertical lines, crosses, and circles in pictures.

• Use correct hand grasp but position on instrument still inconsistent; copy a square and some letters (from first and last name); draw suns; draw human figures, a head with facial features (placement of eye, nose, mouth may not be correct); draw human figures with stick arms and legs and facial parts in correct place; scribble with repeated features and on a horizontal line (looks like writing); scribble leaving space between "words."

• Can form written letters (many inverted or mirror images); color between lines; draw buildings, cars, and boats (proportions incorrect—people are larger than the buildings); trees and flowers; draw with correct proportions; incorporate letters into scribbling; write letters of first name (may not write letters in a line); write letters of last name (may not write letters in a line); draw rectangle, circle, and square.

• Hold pencil with fingertips; draw triangles; follow simple mazes; copy most letters (some still inverted); form words with letters (words may run together; words may begin on one line and end on another); write upper- and lowercase letters and numbers 1–10.

• Can space words when writing; print accurately and neatly; copy a diamond correctly; begin to use cursive writing. (7–8 yrs.)

Continuum adapted from McAfee & Leong 2002, 226.
Copyright © 2002 Allyn & Bacon

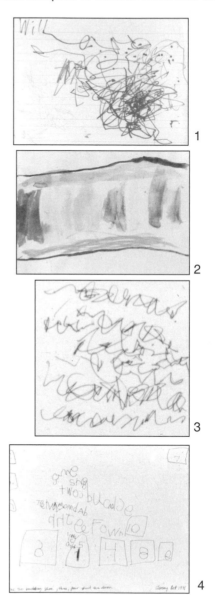

These samples show points in the typical progression in writing ability as described in the developmental continuum:

- Jabs at paper, scribbles with whole arm movement
- Uses horizontal and vertical lines
- Scribbles, sometimes making random strings of letter-like forms and using wavy lines to imitate cursive writing
- Draws circles and squares
- Forms written letters and numerals
- Draws human figures; head with facial features
- Writes letters of first name
- Copies letters (note in #5 how the "Bugle Boy" on the sweatshirt has been reproduced as the child looked down at the shirt he was wearing)
- Forms words with letters; words may run together or begin on one line and end on another (note the invented spelling and use of words to make a sentence)
- Writes upper and lower case letters and numerals
- Spaces words when writing; prints accurately and neatly (note in #9 that Brett makes use of the solid and dotted lines provided as support, but they seem to be of little help to Kaylee in #8)

5

6

7

(samples #8 and #9 on next page)

Figure 10, continued

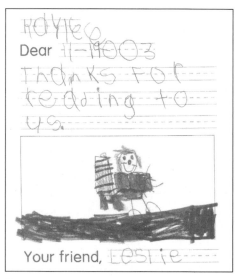

Dear H-19-003
Thanks For
reading to
us.

Your friend, Leslie

8

H-19-03
Dear Leslie
Thank you for coming
to the school.

Your friend, Brett

9

These two thank-you letters, showing the range a teacher could expect within a class, could also be examples of *comparing evidence with expectations.*

If the expected outcome of the curriculum were "Uses conventions in varied forms of written communication (letters, notes, lists,

school papers)," Kaylee's work shows she has a way to go to meet that expectation. She misplaces the recipient's name, the sender's name, and the date, although her message and picture are on target.

Using Your Assessment Information

Like interpretation (the previous step), deciding how to use the assessment information you have gathered calls for sensitivity and drawing on your knowledge of children. Having considered the meaning of the collected evidence, putting information to sound use demands your best professional judgment and the understanding and insight that come from your daily interactions with children. This, too, is a high-level and vital professional activity that teachers engage in.

The most important way we can use assessment results is to help children develop and learn. We do that when we use the information to guide our interactions with children, to engage children with their own learning, and to plan a program to meet children's assessed learning and development needs. As you will see in this section, using assessment information to help children develop and learn links back to the first three of our possible **purposes** for assessing young children. Another important way we can use assessment results links directly to the fourth purpose, which is to report and communicate—for accountability and to families and specialists.

Purposes for assessment—
1. To monitor children's development and learning
2. To guide our planning and decision making
3. To identify children who might benefit from special services
4. To report to and communicate with others

To plan a program to meet assessed needs

Assessment results tell us what children know and can do, as well as which aspects of their learning and development they need more help with. Complicating that picture, the assessed strengths and needs of individual children may be very different from those of the group as a whole. Aligning what we do in the classroom with what assessment reveals is a complex and critical teaching task.

While assessment doesn't spell out our next steps, using assessment information to inform a process of thoughtful, sensitive, and creative curriculum planning is the most powerful use that teachers can make of that information.

This does not mean putting in place a one-size-fits-all plan or scripted lesson plans. Nor does it mean abandoning children's choosing learning centers or activities for assigned, fixed learning groups. Instead, it means that you apply everything you know about how children learn to design a set of learning experiences that will be maximally effective with them. It means knowing the children in your classroom (through assessment) and the expected outcomes of your program (its goals, standards) so well that you can use, shape, modify, or create a curriculum that will help all those children learn and develop. In planning, those three aspects of a quality program—assessment, expected outcomes, curriculum—come together to guide how we meet children's assessed needs.

The subject of how to plan to meet children's learning needs is clearly beyond this booklet's scope. But here are a few useful guidelines about planning in general:

Do whatever planning it takes for you to provide the environment, materials, and interactions with children that will help them learn and thrive. How much planning that will be is individual to you. Some teachers do detailed writing out of their plans; others note only a few reminders. But all teachers need to reflect and plan thoughtfully for the group as a whole and for every individual child.

Involve the entire teaching team. If you share a program with other teachers or paraprofessionals, team planning among members is ideal. Each of you will

How to Use (Not Misuse) Results

Teachers make many important recommendations and decisions about young children and their education, some of which can profoundly affect those children and their families. In that work, we must be guided by solid evidence about children, fully aware of both the possible impacts on their lives and the limitations of assessment.

Many of the ethical concerns relating to assessment arise over the possible misuse of its information. Here are some specific ethical dos and don'ts:

Do assess using multiple measures if the assessment information will be the basis for important educational decisions and recommendations (see NAEYC & NAECS/SDE 2003).

Don't make such important decisions based on just an assessment or two; *never* make them from a single test result.

Do use standardized screening tests only for initial screening and referral for further evaluation. Do link screenings to a follow-up that could provide needed services. Don't use locally developed screening instruments and processes without examining their validity and reliability.

Don't use assessment results to form unchanging ability or skill groups that track children and narrow their opportunities to learn.

Do use assessment results to *individualize* instruction so that it matches today's needs, not yesterday's.

---

contribute your own perspective and ideas and will benefit from the others'. If team planning is not possible, you can plan independently.

Refer to all relevant assessment information as you plan. Study your summary sheets, group checklists, and class profiles for possible clusters of children with like needs, as well as for children's individual needs and accomplishments.

Make sure your planning translates assessment results into individualized activities and action in the classroom. For example, when you are helping children understand the complex concept of relative location, plan to ensure that children who don't know *in, out, next to,* and the concept's other basic words get an opportunity to learn, and those who do are able to use the concept and its words to learn more.

Consult the wealth of guidance available to help you organize your current resources in an intentional fashion to meet children's assessed needs and build on their strengths. Most of the time you do not need "more activities" or "more materials." Instead you may need more specific interactions with specific children (discussed later in this section). Look to professional organizations (e.g., NAEYC, International Reading Association, National Council of Teachers of Mathematics) for general principles and for guides to specific content areas (mathematics, literacy, science) and to development (social-emotional, physical). Other sources are commercial curriculum guides and curriculum guides produced by states, school districts, or programs.

Deliberately incorporate what is being learned in the field of early childhood education (knowledge, strategies) about how to support young children's learning and development. Review your plans to make sure you include new information about such things as children's early literacy acquisition and self-regulation.

Modify the variables that combine to make a learning environment. You can work with, modify, and change most of the variables in your classroom. Time, space, equipment and materials, learning contexts, and adult roles can all be varied to help meet children's assessed needs. For example, almost all activities you do with children can be made simpler or more complex, according to what individual children are ready for.

Make your plans more detailed if the ideas being taught are abstract and complex and if several terms are involved, as in the ideas of relative location, relative size, and likeness/difference.

Include provisions for follow-up in your plan. An activity must be done often enough to allow children to get a solid grasp on the ideas, but not so often to become old. The right interval allows for revisiting and applying important ideas, so children make the ideas theirs. For example, it isn't wise to focus on relative location for a few weeks then drop the concept altogether; instead, plan to keep giving children opportunities to practice words such as *over, under, beside,* and *between.*

Using Assessment to Plan Teaching Strategies: An Example

Goal: To make children's play more sustained and complex.

Assessment of sociodramatic play revealed that 7 of the 19 children in the Mountain View Center's prekindergarten class had difficulty sustaining make-believe play beyond 8–10 minutes.

Play centers were well supplied with materials, and children had both time and encouragement to engage in sustained play, but did not seem to do it. The children were able to make initial plans for a theme (restaurant, doctor's office, beauty shop, house), but could not extend those plans to keep the play going. The inability of these seven children to move to a higher level of play frequently caused a breakdown in play in the groups they were in.

This program sees children's sociodramatic play as a vehicle for increasing the ability to regulate one's own behavior, building oral language skills, and practicing the positive interactions necessary for building friendships, empathy, and social problem solving. The teachers believe that moving toward longer play and episodes of increased complexity would significantly improve the children's progress in those areas.

Because the children are able to initiate the play, they do not need assistance in the early stages, only as the make-believe begins to break down. The teachers plan a three-step intervention to help children extend the play:

• First, the teachers will help the children think of other roles to be incorporated into their original theme.

• If suggesting additional roles is not sufficient to get the children back on track, the teachers will try to help the children extend their own thinking about the play: "What might happen next?" "What might you do if the cook had to go home?" "Who do you suppose might come in next?"

• As a last resort, the teachers will try taking a minor role in the play, but step out once the play gets going again. For example, a teacher might take the role of another customer just wanting a cup of coffee or someone delivering menus.

Armed with these intervention plans, the teachers will be ready to assist the seven youngsters who need help extending and increasing the complexity of their play (and all the other children, too). The teachers will not let the play deteriorate, but neither will they take over. After trying the strategy for a few days, they plan to reassess and make further adjustments if necessary.

Write plans in your planning book or guide. Share the plans with community volunteers and parent helpers so they can help the children too. Plan for these roles, and coach the adults in them as appropriate and needed. Few teachers realize how specific their planning must be when others are involved in using assessment results to help children learn (McAfee & Leong 2002, 141). The helpers who are working with you need to know what to do, how to do it, and why. This is particularly true if you are asking these adults to change the way they have been interacting with children (e.g., if they are to now say "Put those longest blocks on the bottom shelf" instead of "Put them down there").

To guide your interactions with children

Numerous examples throughout this booklet describe ways teachers might change their interactions in response to the assessment information they gather. Changes can include asking questions in a different way, extending an experience for several of the children, supplying different materials, posing a task that is more or less challenging than we had planned, giving different instructions, breaking a concept or skill into smaller steps or pieces (for all or some of the children), slowing down or speeding up, rearranging the physical classroom, and so on. For example, if our assessment tells us that children understand a new word but don't say or use it, we would note that information, and change our questions and requests so children get practice at saying and using the word.

In light of assessment that has children explain their thinking to us, we might reevaluate conclusions we had drawn about what children knew or could do and then make changes. For example, we might ask,

> "Why did you put these animals together and put those in a different pile? I am interested."

> "The d and b do look very much alike. Tell me how they are different."

Sometimes what we thought was evidence of a gap in children's understanding turns out not to be, once the child explains his or her perspective.

We also can use classroom assessment information to identify particular children who need our special attention. If we find that a certain child isn't being sufficiently challenged, we can give her learning experiences that are more demanding. Or if a certain child is falling behind, we can provide him with a larger share of our attention and think of different ways to engage him.

Assessment allows us to support and extend a child's learning at those times and in those ways that mean the most to that child. For example, a skilled teacher:

> Knowing from assessment that some or all of the children don't understand *less than*, might choose a favorite book that includes the term, and use the reading of it to engage them in learning the meaning.

> Will say "Let's go through that again" when some children clearly do not understand—and will change words and actions so they do understand.

> Might pick up on whatever portion of a child's answer was correct or relevant—even *remotely* so—and use that part as a stepping stone to a correct answer.

> Can judge when to quit, when a child needs to work independently for a while and digest new concepts or information.

We use our assessment results to identify just the right kind and amount of support a particular child or group of children needs.

To engage children with their own learning

You can begin to use assessment to help children become active participants in their own learning by replacing stickers, smiley faces, and overused generalities such as "Great job," "Super," and "Good work" with specific information about what the child did that was interesting, significant, or creative to make the work great, super, and good.

You also enhance children's engagement when, instead of just marking "Right" or "Wrong" on their work papers, you help children figure out for themselves what they do and do not understand. It is in this effort that careful assessment and understanding of what children have learned are helpful. A skilled teacher might say,

> "Look at the repeating pattern you made as you built this road."

"You wrote your name all by yourself. Let me show you—if you start in the upper left corner next time, up here, you will have enough room. I'll put a dot there to help you remember."

"Let's look at these three addition problems to see if we can figure out why you found different answers than I did."

When children think about their actions—what they did and why they did it—they are *reflecting*. You can help them develop such reflective (or "metacognitive thinking") skills by giving them the opportunity and time they need for such thinking and by making sensitive requests.

"Tell me why you want this to go in your portfolio."

"What problems did you have while you were doing this? How did you deal with them?"

"Why did you choose this topic to write about?"

"If you were going to build this skyscraper tomorrow, what would you do first?"

To report to and communicate with others

Local programs accountable to funding, governing, and regulatory agencies usually have little or no choice about what assessment information they must report, the way it is reported, or how it is used. (They can and should, however, add other types of assessment for their own purposes.) As educators we have a greater measure of control over the way we use information to communicate with families and specialists.

For accountability

Much accountability information is combined with reports from other schools and centers and becomes public information, available to everyone. Sometimes it is posted on the Internet, sometimes it is headlined in newspapers and on television. It is a good idea to know how your accountability assessment will be reported so you can explain its meaning to families and other interested people.

Families

Sharing information with family members about what their child knows and is able to do can be one way to build a true partnership with them. If you have worked with families as one of the sources of information for assessment—and you should—you have already exchanged assessment information through discussions, notes, and other informal means.

In addition, most schools and centers have their own customary ways of sharing child assessment information. Family conferences, informal reports, written progress reports, and portfolios of children's work are typical for prekindergarten and kindergarten children. Formal progress reports, including report cards, are usually added in the primary grades. Many schools involve children in conferences, sometimes with their portfolios providing a focus for the discussion.

Select only a few things to focus on in a family conference. Make sure that some items are positive and supportive of what the child has learned and can do. Explain in clear and simple language any assessment terms family members may not be familiar with. They may be highly skilled in other disciplines, but do not assume that they know and understand child assessment processes and terms such as *standard, work product, criterion-referenced, developmental level, percentile,* and *proficient.*

The evidence you have collected about children forms the basis for your discussions with parents. Have that evidence organized and ready to use as examples. For example, if you are going to comment on Emily's excellent understanding of mathematics and related skills, bookmark the pages in her portfolio that show that understanding; pull out some anecdotal records, checklists of specific skills, and examples of ways she has helped other children in mathematics. It is not enough to say, "Emily is really good in anything related to math."

If you ask parents to give their child some assistance or extra support in learning at home, be specific about what they can do. For instance, if a child is struggling with reading it does little good to tell his mother to give him "some help." Instead, use assessment results to guide family members in what to do. For example, "Zack really enjoys listening to stories. I am sure he would enjoy and benefit if you read to him for a short time each day. He likes to talk about what he has heard, too."

The wealth of information you have about each child will enable you to talk with families knowledgeably and confidently, as well as to seek their perspectives. They will appreciate that you really know their child.

Specialists

Having assessment information at the ready prepares and empowers us in our work with specialists of all types: speech, hearing, and language therapists; reading, physical, and mental disabilities specialists; psychologists, nurses, social workers.

Teachers are far more likely to be listened to and to get help when they give the specialist relevant examples from classroom assessment, show children's work that illuminates their points, and base their questions on recent well-documented incidents.

If you have a concern about a particular child, collect and record pertinent evidence—the more specific the better. Point out how the evidence applies, if others don't have the classroom experience to see that relationship on their own. If you are involved in team meetings about a child who may need special help, have classroom observations and other documentation ready and organized so you can contribute the classroom perspective to any discussion. Only you and other classroom personnel can contribute information about a child's daily functioning in the classroom.

Making Assessment a Part of Your Classroom

M any people think that the time spent assessing children could be better spent teaching. In this booklet we have tried to show you that assessment does not take away from instruction but instead adds to and improves it. To be an integral part of our efforts to help children develop and learn, assessment should be well planned, systematically implemented, and used appropriately.

Getting started

Making assessment a part of your classroom practice can seem overwhelming at first. Here are some suggestions (adapted from McAfee & Leong 2002, 156–158) to help you get started:

Create a learning environment conducive to ongoing assessment. To ensure that you have time during the day to assess, help children learn to work and play on their own, not just in interaction with an adult. Teach them how to move to their next activity, get help, regulate their own behavior, and solve problems on their own or with their classmates. Children are able to learn that assessment is a regular part of what teachers (and learners) do.

Begin and proceed gradually. Only you know your other personal and professional commitments; prior knowledge and skill; teaching responsibilities; and center, school, and family expectations. You might want to start by assessing one developmental or content area, and focus on it until you feel comfortable with the assessment process. Or start with only four or five children, adding more as you learn. Or don't try to get an anecdotal record on each child each day, but get one on two or three children a day.

Start with easy techniques. Start with assessment techniques that are relatively simple. A checklist would be a good first choice, along with making anecdotal notes about what you see children saying and doing.

Stay organized and current. Many teachers take a few minutes at the end of each day to file away notes, completed charts, and other information. At a minimum, it is important to file once a week. Summarize when there is enough information to warrant it. Keep information current enough to be useful in the classroom. For example, you will need last month's notes to document children's progress, but you need more recent information about what children know and can do to plan tomorrow's or next week's activities.

Enlist the aid of other people. Children, specialists, classroom aides and assistants, volunteers, parents, and interns can help with assessment. Coach all nonprofessionals on confidentiality as well as on what they are to do, and select assessment tasks that are appropriate for them. Children can record their own attendance and participation in centers, write their names on and date their work, and perform numerous other assessment-related tasks. When they do this, they begin to take responsibility for their own learning.

Make assessment a regular, normal part of classroom living. One of the big advantages of the classroom assessment approach is that the normal learning and activities of the classroom do not have to be suspended, as they typically are for screening, readiness, or standardized achievement tests. Instead, in the kind of continuous performance assessment this booklet focuses on, information is collected along the way. The intent is to make gathering and recording information "seem so much a part of the ongoing classroom procedure, so focused on [children's] learning" that the children are hardly aware of it (Almy & Genishi 1979, 9).

Claiming your reward

In learning more about how to assess young children, we have the opportunity for professional and personal growth. We are learning new ideas, trying to figure out where they fit together, and struggling to master new skills and to be objective about the highly personal process of teaching. We may find ourselves questioning prior convictions about children's learning as evidence we collect raises doubts. We may even find that we do not like what assessment results reveal.

You may want to keep a journal to record your triumphs and frustrations. You may want to share these with colleagues as you work together to improve assessment practices at your school or center. Or you may want to keep them as a chronicle of your private growth experiences. But do take advantage of the opportunity to learn how professionally and personally satisfying and rewarding it is to know enough about each of the children in your class to plan experiences that are "just right."

Resources

References

Airasian, P.W. 2000. *Classroom assessment: A concise approach.* 2d ed. Boston: McGraw-Hill.

Almy, M. 1959. *Ways of studying children: A manual for teachers.* New York: Teachers College Press.

Almy, M., & C. Genishi. 1979. *Ways of studying children: An observation manual for early childhood teachers.* Rev. ed. New York: Teachers College Press.

AERA (American Educational Research Association), APA (American Psychological Association), & NCME (National Council on Measurement in Education). 1999. *Standards for educational and psychological testing.* Washington, DC: AERA.

Bodrova, E., D.J. Leong, D.E. Paynter, & D. Semenov. 2000. *A framework for early literacy instruction: Aligning standards to developmental accomplishments and student behaviors. Pre-K through kindergarten.* Rev. ed. Aurora, CO: Mid-continent Research for Education and Learning (McREL).

Council for Exceptional Children. 1999. *IDEA 1997: Let's make it work.* Arlington, VA: Author.

Hills, T.W. 1992. Reaching potentials through appropriate assessment. In *Reaching potentials. Vol. 1: Appropriate curriculum and assessment for young children,* eds. S. Bredekamp & T. Rosegrant, 43–63. Washington, DC: NAEYC.

McAfee, O., & D.J. Leong. 2002. *Assessing and guiding young children's development and learning.* 3d ed. Boston: Allyn & Bacon.

Meisels, S.J., J.R. Jablon, D.B. Marsden, M.L. Dichtelmiller, & A.B. Dorfman. 2001. *The work sampling system.* New York: Pearson Early Learning.

NAEYC & National Association of Early Childhood Specialists in State Departments of Education (NAECS/SDE). 2003. Early childhood curriculum, assessment, and program evaluation: Building an effective, accountable system in programs for children birth through age 8. Washington, DC: NAEYC. Online at www.naeyc.org/resources/position_statements/positions_intro.asp.

Olson, L. 2004. "All means all." In Count me in: Special education in an era of standards. *Education Week on the Web.* January 8, 2004. Online at www.edweek.org, downloaded Jan. 9, 2004.

For More Information

Publications

Almy, M., & C. Genishi. 1979. *Ways of studying children: An observational manual for early childhood teachers.* **Rev. ed. New York: Teachers College Press.**
Analyzes theory and practice of the 1960s and 1970s, and provides new methods to observe children of diverse backgrounds. Presents techniques to help teachers improve their observation skills and reflect on their teaching practices.

Barr, M.D., D.A. Craig, D. Fisette, & M.A. Syverson. 1999. *Assessing literacy with the Learning Record: A handbook for teachers, grades K–6.* **Portsmouth, NH: Heinemann.**
Presents a framework for translating classroom observations into a standards-based reporting process for K-sixth grade. Teacher narratives, samples of student work, and interviews with parents combine to provide comprehensive evidence of students' progress toward agreed-upon goals and standards. Teachers summarize and record this information, using it both to inform their own teaching and to provide a more uniform and quantifiable record of literacy achievement.

Bredekamp, S., & T. Rosegrant. 1995. *Reaching potentials. Vol. 2: Transforming early childhood curriculum and assessment.* **Washington, DC: NAEYC.**
Basic information and guidelines relating to standards, curriculum, and assessment, followed by specific information in the content areas of mathematics, science, health, visual arts, music, social studies, physical education, and language and literacy.

Cohen, D., V. Stern, & N. Balaban. 1996. *Observing and recording the behavior of young children.* **New York: Teachers College Press.**
Basic, classic guide for observing children and recording the observations.

Council for Exceptional Children (CEC). 1999. *IDEA 1997: Let's make it work.* **3d ed. Arlington, VA: Author.**
Presented in easy-to-read question-and-answer format, this document details the legal aspects of the Individuals with Disabilities Education Act regulations issued in 1999, pertaining to parents, schools, and teachers.

Easley, S.D., & K. Mitchell. 2003. *Portfolios matter: What, where, when, why, and how to use them.* **Markham, ONT, Canada: Pembroke.**
Up-to-date, well-organized guide to portfolio construction and use. Provides a good rationale and practical guidance.

Genishi, C., ed. 1992. *Ways of assessing children and curriculum: Stories of early childhood practice.* **New York: Teachers College Press.**
An early, critical response to the standardized testing of preschool children. Presents alternative and more developmentally appropriate assessment measures, such as observation, note taking, role play, and use of portfolios.

Goodwin, W.L., & L.D. Goodwin. 1993. *Handbook for measurement and evaluation in early childhood education.* **San Francisco: Jossey-Bass.**
A textbook and reference book detailing issues in assessment and evaluation, with reviews of tests and other information geared to early childhood specifically.

Grace, C., & E.F. Shores. 1998. *The portfolio book: A step-by-step guide for teachers.* **Beltsville, MD: Gryphon House.**
Excellent guide to the use of portfolios in the early childhood classroom from people who have been involved with portfolio construction from the beginning.

Gronlund, G., & B. Engel. 2001. *Focused portfolios: A complete assessment for the young child.* **St. Paul, MN: Redleaf Press.**
Demonstrates how teachers can observe children in the natural early childhood context. Focuses on four areas of development: Favorites, Friends, Family, and Developmental Milestones.

Gullo, D.F. 1994 (2d ed. in press). *Understanding assessment and evaluation in early childhood education.* **New York: Teachers College Press.**
Explains different assessment and evaluation techniques, their strengths and weaknesses, and when and how they should be applied. Includes helpful glossary and annotated list of selected assessment instruments. New edition covers issues related to standards, children with special needs, and diversity.

Hart, D. 1994. *Authentic assessment: A handbook for educators.* **New York: Addison-Wesley.**
Focuses on why educators are seeking alternative assessments, and how those strategies work in the classroom. Although the book does not concentrate on

early childhood, it does clearly explain basic principles and concepts of good assessment

Helm, J.H., S. Beneke, & K. Steinheimer. 1997. *Windows on learning: Documenting young children's work*. New York: Teachers College Press.
An interesting integration of the Work Sampling System approach to assessment with Reggio Emilio. Offers examples and step-by-step guidelines on how to collect, analyze, and display children's work. Illustrates how to develop individualized portfolios and meet current demands for accountability.

Hills, T.W. 1992. Reaching potentials through appropriate assessment. In *Reaching potentials. Vol. 1: Appropriate curriculum and assessment for young children*, eds. S. Bredekamp & T. Rosegrant, 43–63. Washington, DC: NAEYC.
Shows the connection between assessment and curriculum and provides examples of appropriate assessment strategies that conform to NAEYC and NAECS/SDE curriculum and assessment guidelines.

Hills, T.W. 1993. Assessment in context: Teachers and children at work. *Young Children* 48 (5): 20–28.
Assessment works best when it is integrated into the overall program, it contributes positively to children's self-esteem and developmental process, and it recognizes children's individuality and respects their backgrounds.

Jablon , J.R., A.L. Dombro, & M.L. Dichtelmiller. 1999. *The power of observation*. Washington, DC: Teaching Strategies.
This practical text explores the connection between observing and good teaching. The authors offer many examples that show how to observe effectively and how to use the information gathered to enhance teaching and learning.

Katz, L.G. 1997. A developmental approach to assessment of young children. *ERIC Digest* ERIC ED 407172.
Educators must consider the purposes, risks, and limitations of assessment; recognize the limitations of certain types of assessment; and involve children in evaluating classroom community.

Keyser, D.J., & R.C. Sweetland. 1987–2003. *Test critiques*. Kansas City, MO: Test Corporation of America.
These test critiques contain essential information about a given test, including reliability and validity. Only some of the tests are applicable to early childhood. Updated annually.

Koralek, D., ed. 2004. *Spotlight on young children and assessment.* **Washington, DC: NAEYC.**

A straightforward and accessible booklet to help increase understanding of child assessment and its specialized vocabulary. Provides an overview of basic assessment concepts with a focus on children's development and learning.

Krechevsky, M. 1998. *Project spectrum: Preschool assessment handbook.* **Project Zero Frameworks for Early Childhood Education, vol. 3, eds. H. Gardner, D.H. Feldman, & M. Krechevsky. New York: Teachers College Press.**

Provides the critical means to assess children's cognitive development in the classroom. Includes observation sheets for multiple intelligences.

Kuhs, T.M., R.L. Johnson, S.A. Agruso, & D.M. Monrad. 2001. *Put to the test: Tools and techniques for classroom assessment.* **Portsmouth, NH: Heinemann.**

Gives step-by-step procedures for aligning assessment with standards and provides information about a wide variety of assessment techniques for the K-12 classroom.

Lidz, C.S. 2003. *Early childhood assessment.* **New York: John Wiley & Sons.**

A step-by-step approach to the comprehensive psychological assessment of young children.

McAfee, O., & D.J. Leong. 2002. *Assessing and guiding young children's development and learning.* **3d ed. Boston: Allyn & Bacon.**

Develops both theoretical and practical aspects of child assessment in the early childhood classroom. Covers the many ways to conduct assessment, to document the results of assessments, and to interpret and use the results in the classroom. Developmental continuum charts, organizational guides, and many illustrations guide teachers in setting up a systematic assessment program.

Meisels, S.J. 1999. Assessing readiness. In *The transition to kindergarten,* **eds. R.C. Pianta & M.J. Cox, 39-66. Baltimore, MD: Brookes.**

Addresses interpretations of "readiness" and discusses methods used to assess children's learning at the beginning of formal schooling.

Meisels, S.J., with S. Atkins-Burnett. 1994. *Developmental screening in early childhood: A guide.* **4th ed. Washington, DC: NAEYC.**

How to organize and conduct an exemplary early childhood screening program. Includes advice on selecting an appropriate screening instrument, sample forms, and NAEYC's 1987 position statement on standardized testing.

Meisels, S.J., & E. Fenichel, eds. 1996. *New visions for the developmental assessment of infants and young children.* Washington, DC: Zero to Three/National Center for Infants, Toddlers, and Families.
Promotes a comprehensive approach to assessment building on children's strengths and capabilities, not deficits. Encourages understanding of the challenges children face regarding their families, communities, and culture.

Meisels, S.J., H.L. Harrington, P. McMahon, M.L. Dichtelmiller, & J.R. Jablon. 2001. *Thinking like a teacher: Using observational assessment to improve teaching and learning.* Boston: Allyn & Bacon.
Useful for preservice teachers of young children looking for information on curriculum, observation, documentation, and self-assessment.

Mindes, G. 2003. *Assessing young children.* 2d ed. Upper Saddle River, NJ: Prentice Hall.
An accessible book offering preservice teachers a comprehensive overview of assessment of children from birth through age 8, based on the recommendations of professional organizations.

Murphy, L.L., B.S. Plake, J.C. Impara, & R.A. Spies, eds. 2002. *Tests in print VI: An index to tests, test reviews, and literature on specific tests.* Lincoln, NE: Buros Institute of Mental Measurement, University of Nebraska-Lincoln.
A compilation of comprehensive views and reviews of tests. Only some of the tests are applicable to early childhood.

NAEYC & National Association of Early Childhood Specialists in State Departments of Education (NAECS/SDE). 2002. Joint position statement. *Early learning standards: Creating the conditions for success.* Washington, DC: NAEYC.
Outlines the risks and potential benefits of learning standards for young children, then discusses the essential features that make early learning standards effective. Contains a section on ethical and appropriate assessment strategies. Online at www.naeyc.org/resources/position_statements/positions_intro.asp.

NAEYC & National Association of Early Childhood Specialists in State Departments of Education (NAECS/SDE). 2003. Joint position statement. *Early childhood curriculum, assessment, and program evaluation: Building an effective, accountable system in programs for children birth through age 8.* Washington, DC: NAEYC.
Basic guidelines for curriculum and assessment in early childhood programs and a framework for decision making based on knowledge of and theory and research about how young children develop and learn. Online at www.naeyc.org/resources/position_statements/positions_intro.asp.

NAEYC & National Council of Teachers of Mathematics (NCTM). 2002. *Early childhood mathematics: Promoting good beginnings.* **Joint position statement. Washington, DC: NAEYC; and Reston, VA: NCTM.**
This position statement presents best current thinking on mathematics with young children, including a good section on assessment and its relationship to the curriculum. Online at www.naeyc.org/resources/position_statements/positions_intro.asp.

Plake, B.S., J.C. Impara, & R.A. Spies, eds. 2003. *Fifteenth mental measurements yearbook.* **Lincoln, NE: Buros Institute of Mental Measurements, University of Nebraska-Lincoln.**
This standard source of information on tests contains test reviews and information on the reliability and validity of tests. Only some of the tests are applicable to early childhood. Test reviews and other information are also available online at www.unl.edu/buros/.

Popham, W.J. 2000. *Testing! Testing! What every parent should know about school tests.* **Boston: Allyn & Bacon.**
An easy-to-read and easy-to-understand book for parents about the meaning, importance, and pros and cons of tests and other educational assessments.

Popham, W.J. 2002. *Classroom assessment: What teachers need to know.* **3d ed. Boston: Allyn & Bacon.**
Discusses the different aspects, means, and types of assessment. Covers reliability, validity, the absence of bias, the object and means of assessment, and selected-response tests.

Rudner, L.M. 1994. Questions to ask when evaluating tests. *Practical Assessment, Research, & Evaluation* 4 (2): np.
This article details the kinds of questions test users should ask when choosing and using tests. Online at http://PAREonline.net/getvn.asp?v=4&n=2.

Shepard, L.A. 1994. The challenges of assessing young children appropriately. *Phi Delta Kappan* 76 (3): 206–12.
Testing and other assessment measures have often been misused. Assessment advocates must demonstrate the usefulness of assessment and prohibit abuses.

Sutton, J.P., & E.J. Nowacek, eds. 2003. *Assessment of culturally-linguistically diverse learners.* **Reston, VA: Council for Exceptional Children.**
Covers issues related to cultural-linguistic diversity and assessment of early learners, Latino and African American children, gifted and talented children, and second-language learners.

Wortham, S.C. 1996. *The integrated classroom: The assessment-curriculum link in early childhood education.* Englewood Cliffs, NJ: Merrill.
Offers preservice teachers information about integrated classrooms, integration of assessment and learning, and integration of appropriate curriculum and instruction.

Wortham, S.C. 2000. *Assessment in early childhood education.* 3d ed. Upper Saddle River, NJ: Pearson Education.
A survey of the types of assessment that are effective with children from birth to age 8 and how to use them to best advantage. In addition, it includes information on the latest standardized tests, detailed directions for interpreting assessments, and tips for communicating assessment results.

Web sites

The Internet addresses below will get you to the organizations' home pages. From there you can access a variety of current and older resources related to assessment, curriculum, and other topics. Although these organizations are well-established, be aware that Internet availability of resources changes with funding, emphasis of the organization, and current issues in education. The listing below reflects availability at the time of this volume's publication.

Association for Supervision and Curriculum Development (ASCD)— www.ascd.org
ASCD publishes information on topics related to education at all levels, including early childhood. See particularly "A Lexicon of Learning: What Educators Mean When They Say . . . "

Buros Institute of Mental Measurements—www.unl.edu/buros/
Searchable database of tests, but most are not applicable to early childhood education.

CLAS (Culturally and Linguistically Appropriate Services) Early Childhood Research Institute—www.clas.uinc.edu
Collects a wide variety of early childhood and early intervention resources for children and families from diverse cultural and linguistic backgrounds.

Council for Exceptional Children (CEC)—www.cec.sped.org
The Council for Exceptional Children is an authoritative source for information about assessment of children with special needs.

Council of Chief State School Officers (CCSSO)—www.ccsso.org
CCSSO has projects focusing on early childhood and general educational issues. Look for a glossary of assessment-related terms specific to early childhood at www.ccsso.org/eceaglossary.

Early Childhood and Parenting (ECAP) Collaborative—http://ecap.crc.uiuc.edu/info
Source for public domain materials formerly collected and distributed by ERIC's Clearinghouse on Elementary and Early Childhood Education (ERIC/EECE), including *Eric Digests* and other publications.

Educational Testing Service (ETS)—www.ets.org
The Educational Testing Service makes available many resources on assessment. The test collection contains more than 20,000 tests, including more than 80 early childhood tests and assessments. The test collection is designed for researchers, graduate students, and teachers.

National Association for the Education of Young Children (NAEYC)—www.naeyc.org
NAEYC makes all its position papers available online (some also can be purchased in booklet format). Recommendations on assessment, standards, and curriculum are available. Assessment-related articles from the *Young Children* journal are also available online.

National Center for Research on Evaluation, Standards, and Student Testing (CRESST)—www.cse.ucla.edu
This site has authoritative information on standards, assessment, and testing, plus a wide variety of information pertaining to all aspects of assessment in education.

National Clearinghouse for English Language Acquisition and Language Instruction Educational Programs—www.ncela.gwu.edu
This site is funded by the U.S. Department of Education's Office of English Language Acquisition (OELA). It collects, analyzes, and disseminates information relating to the education of linguistically and culturally diverse learners in the United States.

National Institute for Early Education Research—www.nieer.org
NIEER makes available information on current research relating to early childhood education, including standards, assessment, and curriculum. A question-and-answer service is available. Users can search an Internet database on pre-K assessments by type of test, domain covered, reliability, and validity.

Practical Assessment, Research, and Evaluation—http://pareonline.net/
   Home.htm
Provides education professionals access to refereed articles that can have a positive
impact on assessment, research, evaluation, and teaching practice, especially at the
local education agency (LEA) level. (Site used to be part of the ERIC Clearinghouse
on Assessment and Evaluation.)

SearchERIC.org—http://edresearch.org
Current site for the abstracts and *Digests* of the former ERIC Clearinghouse on
Assessment and Evaluation. The site has links to many other sites that describe
assessment, issues in assessment, and basic information about assessment. It also
makes available an online journal on practical assessment.

U.S. Department of Education—www.ed.gov
The official Web site of the U.S. Department of Education has many resources
related to assessment, particularly in public school settings.

Glossary

Terms in **bold** are defined in this Glossary.

accommodation—A change in assessment procedures that allows the child to participate in the assessment but that does *not* alter what the assessment measures or its comparability. [compare with **modification**]

accountability—Being held responsible for something. In early childhood education, teachers and programs are typically held accountable for meeting a **standard** of performance. Can include being held accountable for child outcomes.

achievement test—A **standardized test** that assesses how much content (knowledge and skills) a child has learned compared with other children of the same age or grade level.

align—To line up, be consistent with, or get into position with. Once expectations for learning are agreed on, the curriculum should align with those expectations; that is, the curriculum should teach children the things they will be expected to have learned. Assessment should align with both outcomes and the curriculum, measuring what the outcomes specify and what the curriculum teaches.

alternative assessment—[see **performance assessment**]

artifact—[see **work product**]

assessment (or **child assessment**)—A term sometimes used loosely to refer to any type of appraisal of young children. In a narrower sense, assessment refers to information from multiple **indicators** and sources of **evidence** that is organized and interpreted and then evaluated to make an appraisal.

authentic assessment (or **direct assessment**)—A type of **performance assessment** that uses tasks that are as close as possible to real-life practical and intellectual challenges. Specifically, refers to the *situation or context* in which the task is performed; that is, the child completes the desired behavior in a context as close to real life as possible. [see also **performance assessment**]

benchmark (or **milestone**)—A point of reference for measurement and **evaluation**. Used especially in connection with **content standards**. Usually more specific than a **standard**, giving more details about performance.

bias—Any characteristic of an assessment that unfairly discriminates against or favors a child or a group of children on the basis of factors such as gender, urban or rural residence, socioeconomic class, ethnic origin, culture, or language.

child assessment—[see **assessment**]

classroom assessment (or **classroom-embedded assessment**)—Assessments developed and used by teachers in their classrooms on a day-to-day basis. [see also **curriculum-embedded assessment**]

content standard—An outcome statement that specifies *what* every child should know and be able to do. [see also **performance standard**]

context—Refers to the entire situation in which the assessment is given. Context includes such things as the environment (in a classroom, in a special room), how and by whom questions are asked or requests are made, and how the child answers (paper-pencil, points to, speaks, demonstrates).

criterion—A specific level or cut-off score for acceptable performance.

criterion-referencing—A means of determining where a child stands compared with a **criterion** or with a **performance standard**, rather than compared with other children. [compare with **norm-referencing**]

> **criterion-referenced standardized test**—A **standardized test** in which a child's score is compared with a **criterion**. [compare with **norm-referenced standardized test**]

curriculum-embedded assessment—Assessment that is integrated as part of the curriculum, in contrast to **tests** or other assessments that are given apart from daily teaching and instruction. The teacher assesses the children using the classroom activity itself and not a separate procedure.

desired outcome—[see **standard**]

developmental continuum—A predictable but not rigid sequence of the knowledge or skill levels typically achieved or attained by young children.

developmental rating scale (or **developmental profile**)—An assessment that compares a child's performance with a set of developmental **norms** established through research.

developmentally appropriate—Regarding practices, including assessment, that are *age* appropriate, *culturally* appropriate, and *individually* appropriate for each child.

diagnostic evaluation (or **diagnostic assessment**)—An in-depth appraisal of a child by a specialist to identify specific abilities and needs, frequently administered after the child has been noticed in a **screening** or by a teacher or family member.

direct assessment—[see **authentic assessment**]

documentation—The record made of **evidence** of what a child or group of children have done or accomplished.

documenting—The process of systematically gathering information about what children have done or accomplished. Consists of finding out, then making a record.

domain—An area of development, usually including psychomotor development, cognitive development, and affective development.

evaluation—The process of making a judgment about assessment results, applying some value. Evaluation is sometimes considered a different task from assessment, but is frequently included as the *last* step in assessment.

evidence—An outward sign or indication. In **child assessment,** evidence would be an outward sign about a child's development and learning; for example, an *observation* of how long a child spent "reading" books, a *drawing* on which a child printed his own name using correct letter forms, or a parent's *account* of a child's persistent questioning "What's that letter?"

expectation—[see **standard**]

formal assessment—A term with a wide variety of meaning, typically describing assessment used for the purpose of reporting to others. There are often specific requirements for a formal assessment, such as using **standardized** procedures for all children, following a specific format, or using a specific **instrument.** Examples might vary from **classroom assessments** that use a specific set of **scoring rubrics** to **standardized tests.** [compare with **informal assessment**]

frequency—The number of times that something, such as a behavior or a specific answer, occurs.

high-stakes assessment—An assessment that has the potential to influence important educational decisions made about programs, teachers, or children. High-stakes assessment for children might influence placement in special programs, ability grouping, or retention in grade.

indicator—**Evidence** that documents children's attainment of a specific level of a **benchmark** or **standard**.

informal assessment—A term with a wide variety of meaning. Could be used to describe information collected for the teacher's use only (e.g., to make classroom decisions or adjustments to instruction) that might or might not be written or follow a specific format. Could also be used to describe any method of gathering information in the classroom that is not a **standardized test**. Although informal assessments might not be highly accurate or consistent from child to child, they can yield useful insights into children's learning. [compare with **formal assessment**]

instrument (or **tool**)—A systematic means of collecting and recording information about young children. Examples include a checklist, **performance assessment,** and rating scale. Can also refer to a **standardized test** that is published and meets testing standards.

milestone—[see **benchmark**]

modification—A change in assessment procedures that *does* alter what the assessment measures and the comparability of results. [compare with **accommodation**]

multiple measures—Refers to having gathered information from different sources, in different settings or **contexts,** and recording that information using different methods.

narrative record—Any of several kinds of records that describe children's behavior. Examples include anecdotal records, jottings, and annotations.

norming group—The group of children used to establish the scoring system for a **standardized test.**

norm-referencing—A means of determining where a child's performance stands compared with the performances of other children on the same measure. The meaning of the score emerges from comparison with the average score calculated from scores that the **norming group** of children obtained on that test. [compare with **criterion-referencing**]

> **norm-referenced standardized test**—A **standardized test** in which the child's score is compared with other children's scores. [compare with **criterion-referenced standardized test**]

objective—[see **standard**]

observation (or **observational measurement**)—A method of gathering information by systematically watching and noting what children do and say.

outcome—Changes in behavior, knowledge, understanding, ability, skills, and/or attitudes that are expected as a result of participating in a program or course of study, receiving services, or using a product.

percentile rank—A way of reporting a child's score on a **standardized test.** Percentile rank describes what percentage of the children in the **norming group** had the same or a lower score than the child's score. For example, a child in the 90th percentile scored the same as or better than 90 percent of the children who took the test.

performance assessment (or **performance-based assessment, alternative assessment**)—Finding out what children know and can do from their ability to perform certain tasks. Usually uses tasks as close as possible to real-life practical and intellectual challenges. Specifically refers to the *type of response* by the child; e.g., if writing is being assessed, the child writes. [see also **authentic assessment**]

performance standard—An outcome statement that specifies *how well* a child should demonstrate knowledge and skills; it gauges the degree to which the child has met a **content standard.**

portfolio—A purposeful collection of the child's work and other **indicators** of learning, collected over time, that demonstrates to the child and to others the child's efforts, progress, or achievement in particular developmental or subject area(s).

portfolio assessment—A type of assessment that evaluates a child's performance based on **evidence** that the teacher and the child have selected and compiled in a **portfolio.**

program evaluation (or **program assessment**)—A process that looks at factors relating to the quality of the classroom or other care setting. Those factors might include available equipment and supplies, teacher qualifications, square footage, adult:child ratios and interactions, and parent involvement. Program evaluation may or may not include information gathered about the children who are in the program.

qualitative assessment—Assessment that is descriptive, that gathers information that describes the *quality* of the child's performance. Examples include a **narrative record** or **scoring rubric.** [compare with **quantitative assessment**]

quantitative assessment—Assessment that measures the **frequency** of a child's behavior, its duration, or assigns the behavior a rating. Examples include a count, tally, checklist, participation chart, scan, rating scale, ranking, and **rubric**. [compare with **qualitative assessment**]

readiness test—A test to evaluate whether or not a student is ready for a particular academic program. School readiness tests are **standardized tests** given to children before, at the time of entering, or in the first few months of kindergarten to measure knowledge and skills related to school learning and to predict school success. (There is widespread concern about the misuse of readiness tests and about the ability of these tests to predict school success.)

referral—The recommendation that a child receive further **diagnostic evaluation** or special services.

reflection (or **self-reflection**)—A process of thoughtfully considering an experience, idea, work product, or learning. It is a thoughtful "looking back" that usually involves language and may lead to revision based on the reflection.

reliability—The extent to which any assessment technique yields results that are accurate and consistent over time. Assessments with high reliability are described as "reliable."

response—What the child does to answer a question or solve a problem presented by the assessment. A child's response can be either "constructed" or "selected." In a constructed response, children are asked to recall, combine, and apply their knowledge and skills in a response they build from scratch. In a selected response children are asked to choose the correct answer from a limited range of options.

rubric—A rule or guide presenting clear criteria by which a complex performance (e.g., thinking critically or writing) can be judged. Designates a special type of rating scale used as a guide in evaluating specific qualities of children's performances.

sampling—Assessing a part of the population instead of the entire population, or a part of a domain of learning instead of the entire domain.

scoring rubric—A fixed scale and a list of characteristics describing performance for each of the points on the scale. Usually one of the various points is denoted as being an acceptable level of performance.

screening—Brief, relatively inexpensive, **standardized** procedures or **tests** designed to quickly appraise a large number of children to find out which ones need further evaluation.

standard (n.) (or **expectation, objective, desired outcome, criterion**)—An outcome statement that specifies what children should know and be able to do. [see also **content standard, performance standard**]

standard (adj.) (or **standardized**)—When the same procedure is used to collect information from all of the children. To ensure fairness in testing from one child to the next, children are asked to answer the same question or to do the same task. Can mean having the same time limitations for completing the assessment, giving a specific set of directions, or following specific steps in administering the assessment.

standardized—[see **standard** (adj.)]

standardized test—A **test** with specific characteristics: (1) developed according to American Psychological Association/American Educational Research Association guidelines, with high levels of **reliability** and **validity**; (2) prescribed methods for administration and security; and (3) scoring systems based on comparisons either with other test takers (**norm-referencing**) or with a specified level of performance (**criterion-referencing**). Not all **tests** that are published and available for public use meet these requirements to be labeled "standardized."

structured performance—A situation in which a specific set of questions or a task is used to elicit what the child knows and can do.

test—A systematic procedure for **sampling** a child's behavior and knowledge that usually summarizes the child's performance by a score. Tests can be oral or written, **norm-** or **criterion-referenced.** The results of the test are used to make generalizations about the child's total knowledge and skills. [see also **achievement test, readiness test, screening, standardized test**]

tool—[see **instrument**]

validity—The extent to which an assessment measures what we want to measure and not something else. An assessment is "valid" if the results agree with other information gathered in other ways about the same behavior.

work product (or **artifact**)—Tangible items that result from children's work and play that give **evidence** of their learning. Examples are drawings, paintings, writing samples, block buildings, graphs, and arithmetic papers.

Early years are learning years

Become a member of NAEYC, and help make them count!

Just as you help young children learn and grow, the National Association for the Education of Young Children—your professional organization—supports you in the work you love. NAEYC is the world's largest early childhood education organization, with a national network of local, state, and regional Affiliates. We are more than 100,000 members working together to bring high-quality early learning opportunities to all children from birth through age eight.

Since 1926, NAEYC has provided educational services and resources for people working with children, including:

• *Young Children*, the award-winning journal (six issues a year) for early childhood educators

• **Books, posters, brochures, and videos** to support your work with young children and families

• **The NAEYC Annual Conference**, which brings tens of thousands of people together from across the country and around the world to share their expertise and ideas on the education of young children

• **Insurance plans** for members and programs

• **A voluntary accreditation system** to help programs reach national standards for high-quality early childhood education

• **Young Children International** to promote global communication and information exchanges

• **www.naeyc.org**—a dynamic Web site with up-to-date information on all of our services and resources

To join NAEYC

To find a complete list of membership benefits and options or to join NAEYC online, visit **www.naeyc.org/membership.** Or you can mail this form to us.

(Membership must be for an individual, not a center or school.)

Name _____

Address _____

City_____ State_____ ZIP_____

E-mail_____

Phone (H)_____ (W)_____

❏ New member ❏ Renewal ID # _____

Affiliate name/number _____

To determine your dues, you must visit **www.naeyc.org/membership** or call 800-424-2460, ext. 2002.

Indicate your payment option

❏ VISA ❏ MasterCard

Card #_____

Exp. date _____

Cardholder's name _____

Signature _____

Note: By joining NAEYC you also become a member of your state and local Affiliates.

Send this form and payment to

NAEYC, PO Box 97156, Washington, DC 20090-7156